ABC Basic
Chart Reading

Lynne Palmer

ISBN-10: 0-86690-136-1
ISBN-13: 978-0-86690-136-9

Cover Design: Jack Cipolla

Published by:
American Federation of Astrologers, Inc.
6535 S. Rural Road
Tempe, AZ 85283

www.astrologers.com

Printed in the United States of America

Contents

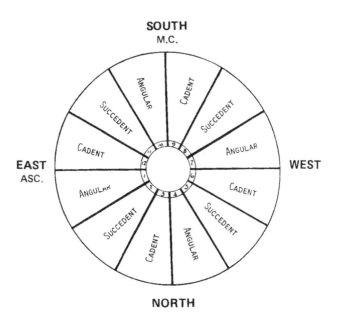

Zodiacal Sign	Planetary Ruler
♈ Aries	♂ Mars
♉ Taurus	♀ Venus
♊ Gemini	☿ Mercury
♋ Cancer	☽ Moon
♌ Leo	☉ Sun
♍ Virgo	☿ Mercury
♎ Libra	♀ Venus
♏ Scorpio	♇ Pluto and ♂ Mars
♐ Sagittarius	♃ Jupiter
♑ Capricorn	♄ Saturn
♒ Aquarius	♅ Uranus and ♄ Saturn
♓ Pisces	♆ Neptune and ♃ Jupiter

ASPECT	DEG	SYM	CADENT		SUCCEDENT		ANGULAR	
			P	L	P	L	P	L
SEMISEXTILE	30°	⊻	1°	2°	2°	3°	3°	4°
SEMISQUARE	45	∠	3	4	4	5	5	6
SEXTILE	60	⚹	5	6	6	7	7	8
SQUARE	90	□	6	8	8	10	10	12
OPPOSITION	180	☍	8	11	10	13	12	15

SYM	DEG	ASPECT
⊼	150°	INCONJUNCT
⊡	135	SESQUISQUARE
⚹	60	SEXTILE
△	120	TRINE
☌	0	CONJUNCTION

How to Use This Book

The horoscope maps the native's specific attitude toward an event, situation, person, hobby and/or vocation. In *Horoscope of Billy Rose*, I wrote: "In astrological delineation, combining planetary aspects, their house positions, strength and power with the personal conditioning and environment gives a picture of the complete individual."

Two people may have the same aspect in their horoscopes, but due to their conditioning, they may react differently. One individual may use the harmonious traits of a discordant aspect, whereas another person may use the discordant traits of the same aspect.

In astrology you should gear the aspect to work the way that *you* will benefit. Do not allow the aspects (and planets) to rule you. Instead, you should rule them!

Aspects

Aspects represent energy outlets. They indicate the type of harmonious or discordant energy that is present at a specific time.

The *harmonious aspects* indicate the areas of life (the houses) where it is easier to accomplish the matters attracted (the matters ruled by the houses and planets) through using the harmonious expressions of the planets involved in the aspect.

Under harmonious aspects you don't feel the need to do things or that you must do anything. Therefore, you must push yourself because there is a tendency to be lazy.

The *discordant aspects* indicate the areas of life (the houses) where it is difficult to accomplish the matters ruled by the houses and planets. This is because it is natural to use the discordant expressions of the planets involved in the aspect.

Under discordant aspects you feel driven to accomplish things. You feel *you must* take action. You may have a struggle, but you will at least make an attempt to do something.

The discordant aspects indicate the type of problem that an individual has. For example:

Do you have a semisquare aspect? Is your problem one of annoyance? If so, what is annoying you? What areas of life (houses) are annoying you? What type of thinking and acting is causing the annoyances? (This is indicated by the meaning of the planets.) Is the annoyance in relation to your hobby and/or job? If so, the houses involved in the aspect and/or the type of vocation ruled by the planet will indicate the areas of work or hobby that cause an annoyance.

In many instances an individual will have both harmonious and discordant aspects during the same time period by major progression. In this case it is possible to be driven (under the discordant aspects) to accomplish something and to be successful as a result (under the harmonious aspects).

Houses

The house will indicate the department of life that is involved in the aspect. The matters listed under a particular house will not *all* be expressed simultaneously, and so you must eliminate as many of the matters (listed under the houses) as possible. This is where having the case history of an individual is important. If you know the areas a person is involved in, it is easier to give a reading; however, a reading *can* be given without this information. Instead of eliminating areas, you would say, "If you are involved in this area . ., or this area . ., or this area . .," etc.

If a house is discordant during a specific time period (as implied by major progressions), it is sometimes better to avoid the areas of life that are involved in the aspect. For example, if you invest money in the stock market (fifth house) and you have only discordant aspects with the planets that rule the fifth house, it is unwise to invest during the time period. It is too risky and a loss will probably be the result of such an investment. During the same time period, it is wise to focus on the departments of life (the houses) where you have harmonious aspects.

There are individuals who thrive when under a challenge, people who reject what is easy and enjoy when going into dangerous areas . . . "where angels fear to tread."

The horoscope chart is a wheel with twelve spokes. The spokes are the house cusp dividing lines, and they divide one house from another. On the outer edge of each spoke is a sign of the zodiac with its degrees and minutes. This sign is ruled by a planet, or by two planets in the case of double rulership. (See diagrams on pages iv and v.)

A chart may have many areas (houses) that are empty. These empty areas are as easily read as those that have a planet(s) in a house. The empty area of life is not as important to the individual as the area where there is a planet. The natal position of the planet and its major progressed position are the most important areas to an individual.

House Rulerships

A planet, or planets, in a house rule that house. Where there is only one planet in a house, it is always the chief ruler of the house. The planet (or planets in the case of double rulership, such as Aquarius, which is ruled by Saturn and Uranus) ruling the zodiacal sign on the house cusp is the co-ruler (or co-rulers) of the house. If there is more than one planet in a house, the planet *nearest* (in degrees and minutes) *to the house cusp* it is in is the chief ruler. The planet in the house *next nearest* (in degrees and minutes) *to the house cusp* is the first co-ruler. If there are more planets, they become second, third, etc. co-rulers. The last ruler of the house is the planet (or planets in the case of double rulership) ruling the zodiacal sign on the house cusp. If there is an intercepted sign, the planet (or planets in the case of double rulership) ruling that zodiacal sign would be the last rulers of that house.

Many charts have five or more planets ruling a house. For example, say the Sun, Mercury and Mars are in Aquarius in the sec-

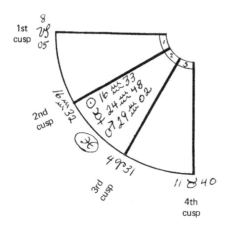

1st cusp ♉ 05

2nd cusp 16 ♒ 32

3rd cusp 4 ♈ 31

16 ♒ 33
⊙ 24 ♒ 48
☿ 7 ♓ 19 ♒ 02
♇

11 ♉ 40
4th cusp

Figure 1

ond house, and Aquarius is on the house cusp with Pisces intercepted in the house. Aquarius has a double rulership, with both Uranus and Saturn ruling this sign. Pisces has a double rulership of Neptune and Jupiter.

Looking at Figure 1, the second house would have the following as chief ruler and co-rulers: chief ruler is the Sun, because it is nearer the second house cusp. The first co-ruler is Mercury because it is next nearest the house cusp. The second co-ruler is Mars because its degrees and minutes are higher (larger) than Mercury's. The next co-rulers are Saturn and Uranus because these planets are co-rulers of Aquarius, which is on the second house cusp. The last co-rulers are Neptune and Jupiter, co-rulers of Pisces, which is intercepted in the second house.

Planets

In this book you will notice that I have listed many words or sentences that have the same meaning. This is representative of the different words people use to express the same thing. Therefore, you can use the word of your choice as long as it has the same meaning. If the person whose horoscope you are reading to does not understand your words, change them to words that the person can identify with. Communication is most vital in astrology.

In some cases, you will discover one word listed under a planet and later discover the same word listed under another planet. For example, the word *antagonistic* appears under the discordant side of Mars and Pluto. This implies that a competitive, tempestuous and angry *reaction* to *antagonistic* feelings *is* expressed by Mars. The forceful, hostile and mutually bad feeling as a reaction to *an-*

tagonistic feelings is expressed by Pluto. It takes various actions and traits to become involved *in* a specific reaction, act, thought, feeling, or vocation. If one knows and understands all the types of energies required to express a particular thing, there is no problem in locating the planets for that specific area.

One person may *not* use *all* of the traits or actions listed, or become involved in *all* of the hobbies and/or occupations listed under a planet. The stronger and more dominant (see *How to Read Cosmodynes* by Doris Chase Doane for a discussion of dominant planets) the planet is in the chart, the more pronounced the actions, traits, hobbies and/or work will be for that individual under that particular planetary heading.

Each planet listed has a harmonious and discordant side. You may become involved in one or more of these hobbies and/or vocations listed. You may express more than one action or trait listed. You may attract people into your life who use these traits and actions, or are involved in the hobbies and/or work listed.

Try to use the positive side of the planet rather than its discordant side. If you notice that you are using the actions and traits *listed* under the discordant side, read the actions and traits expressed on the harmonious side of the planet. Change and adjust your thoughts and actions to the planet's constructive side.

This book may be used for natal, major or minor progressions, or for reading the transits.

On the harmonious side of a planet: one is favored by the type of people involved with the aspect or house involved and through using the traits, actions, hobbies or work listed under the harmonious side of the planet. It is the *way* that you express these traits and actions toward specific areas that makes people desirous of helping you. These areas of occupation are easier to perform.

On the discordant side of a planet: the type of people listed under the planet, and in *relation* to the houses involved in the aspect, may be a source of difficulty. You, or others, and actions listed under the discordant side of the planet will bring problems and people may not be as inclined to assist you. You may attract difficulties, trouble and/or losses involving the houses and with the areas listed under the discordant side of the planet is the *way* that you express actions toward specific areas that make people desirous of running away from you. These areas of occupations are more difficult to perform.

When a planet is discordant it does *not* detract, take away from or imply failure in a given area. The discordant kind of energy, when used discordantly, makes the vocation and/or success more difficult to obtain because there is a struggle. People may try to block you from doing things, or your attitude may form the blockage.

Note: Many of the discordant traits and actions listed under the planets are not very nice. Life embraces all types of people with all types of acting and thinking. Therefore, I have included these negative forces.

ABC Procedure

Memorize the meanings of the aspects, houses and planets. By reading and studying one planet a day, you can understand the overall picture of the planet. Stop and think about all of the people you know and how they have used these energies. Become aware of everyone. When someone talks to you, try to figure out which planet is being expressed.

Procedure

A. Look up the meaning of the aspect in Chapter Two. If the aspect is *harmonious*, read the harmonious side of the planets involved in the aspect in Chapter Three. If the aspect is *discordant*, read the discordant side of the planets involved in the aspect in Chapter Three.

B. Look up the meanings of the houses in which the aspected planets are located and the meanings of the houses whose cusps these two planets rule (see Chapter One).

C. If the aspect is *harmonious*, look up the meanings of the harmonious side of both planets involved in the aspect.

If the aspect is *discordant*, look up the meanings of the discordant side of both planets involved in the aspect.

If the aspect is *neutral*, and the planets are neutral (see page 24). This approach is also applied to the inconjunct aspect and the parallel aspect.

If a *neutral aspect involves Mars, Saturn, Venus or Jupiter*, see page 24 for an explanation.

D. After you have completed the above steps, try putting everything together.

E. Use common sense and logic. For instance, if a person wants to invest in the stock market, care must be taken to choose an appropriate time to take action. Naturally the astrologer would select a time and date when the stock market was open for business. Also, when you have the native's case history, you can eliminate actions and events that are not pictured in the horoscope.

F. How to read aspects that involve the Midheaven and Ascendant: The *Midheaven aspects* refer to the actions, traits, matters, affairs and/or people represented by the tenth house and are read accordingly.

The *Ascendant aspects* refer to the actions, traits, matters, affairs and/or people represented by the first house and are read accordingly.

How to Read an Aspect

This example concerns a man who has the Sun trine the Moon. A trine is harmonious; therefore, read the harmonious Sun and Moon together with the meaning of the trine and also with the meanings of the houses ruled by the Sun and Moon, as follows:

The *Sun* rules his tenth house and is located there. It also rules his ninth house as a co-ruler because the sign Leo is on the ninth house cusp (the Sun rules Leo).

The *Moon* rules the second house and is located there. It also rules his eighth house as a co-ruler because the sign Cancer is on the eighth house cusp (the Moon rules Cancer).

It is with these house areas (second, eighth, ninth and tenth) that he would experience good fortune (trine) if he expresses the harmonious traits and actions ruled by the Sun and the Moon.

A Sun harmonious trait is dependability. The Sun located in the tenth house of profession indicates that when he is dependable regarding business, money can come easily (the money is the Moon ruling the second house, and easily relates to the trine). This money could come through the general public (the Moon), or the retail trade (the Moon) and would enable him to pay his debts (eighth house) and he could travel to foreign countries (ninth house) and make money through that area because of his connections with men (the Sun) in power (the Sun and the tenth house).

Although this brief example can be expanded in order to cover many possibilities, it illustrates the way to begin. Following this ABC procedure will make chart reading easier for you. Good luck!

Lynne Palmer

Chapter One

The Houses

One of the factors interpreted in reading a horoscope refers to the twelve houses. Study the diagram presented at the front of this book. There you will find the numbers on the inner circle representing each house discussed in this chapter.

First House

First House People
Self.
One's makeup, disposition, nature.
One's personal appearance (exclusive, particular and individual physical features, face, image as visibly seen by others).
How one moves about (fast, slow, nervously, etc.).
One's physical body (physique, stature, figure).
The health (well-being, nutrition) of one's physical body.
The vitality of one's physical body (endurance, stamina, strength).

First House Matters
One's exclusive, individual and particular activities which appeal to, fascinate, absorb, concern and engage one's attention.
One's personal undertakings, ventures, pursuits.

One's personal likes, dislikes, habits and life.

One's personal changes (individual remodeling, adapting and revising thoughts and physical structure which changes the appearance, attitude, thinking).

One's own personal concerns, affairs, interests, circumstances.

Second House

Second House People

Bankers.

One that deals with money and/or securities, such as a stockbroker or investment advisor.

Second House Matters

Exclusive and individual money, cash, currency, legal tender.

Actual money earned, gained, lost or spent.

The manner in which one earns, gains, saves or spends cash.

Source of wages, revenue, paycheck or receipts that originate, derive or spring from the result of one's work, business or investments.

Earning capacity (the power, competence and capability of receiving and making money).

Cash on hand.

Bank account, and money one deposits in a checking account.

Personal securities, securities (stocks and bonds in one's name), and personal holdings.

Personal possessions (clothes, furs, jewelry, furniture and material things one owns).

Personal property, such as land, lots, buildings, real estate . . . that which is owned by exclusive rights. Note regarding personal property: The money involved and the possession on paper is the second house. The actual land, buildings and real estate is the fourth house.

Third House

Third House People

Agents (one who acts for another; intermediary, go-between, representative).

Office worker, secretary, stenographer.

Bookkeeper.

Clerk (one who keeps accounts and records).

Correspondent (one who writes letters or regularly provides news for publication).

One who delivers mail, postal worker, postal clerk.

Journalist, reporter.

Copy writer (one who reproduces and transcribes other people's work).

Ghost writer (writing articles or literary works for which another person receives credit).

One who works on land dealing with cars, railroads, buses, trucks and transportation; printer (one who works with any form of communication).

Telephone operator, call center customer service representative.

Flight attendant (one who flies short distance trips).

Blood relatives . . . brother (also half and step-brother), sister (also half and step-sister), aunts, uncles, nieces, nephews, cousins.

Educator.

Third House Matters

Signing contracts, deals, formal agreements, credentials, documents, papers. Correspondence (exchange of letters, messages, notes, memorandums, email and text, and correspondence that one writes, sends, receives, reads).

Conversations (informal or familiar talk, oral discourse or exchange of ideas between people).

News (tidings, report of recent events, something unknown to the listener or reader, news one gives or receives).

Telephone calls, text messages, email.

Communication.

Rumors (hearsay, tall tales, gossip).

Writing in general (article, composition, essay, manuscript, note, letter, novel, thesis, song and/or poetry).

Magazines (periodicals, journals, publications).

Newspapers (daily, weekly).

Ideas (impressions, notions, views, theories, train of thought).

Mediation.

Intellectual activity (mental and conscious).

Expression of one's mental faculties (brain and intellect).

Education (background, learning, instruction).

Private studies (confidential, concealed and secret classes, courses and subjects).

Communication devices (information handling).

Communication satellites.

Keyboarding, data entry, typing.

Mail order (either one who purchases, orders or reserves through mail or one who is in the mail order business and mails items and catalogues to others).

Trips (taking short jaunts, commuting any short distance, with the distance judged by the individual's experience with travel).

Transportation (buses, cabs, cable cars, trolley cars, trains, subways, trucks, automobiles, bicycles, motorcycles).

Fourth House

Fourth House People

Father (also foster or step-father or grandfather) and one's attitude toward the father.

Miner (excavator, digger, burrower).

Farmer (agriculturist, harvester, reaper, sower, grower, raiser, planter, sharecropper, rancher).

Gardener, landscaper, horticulturist.

Landowner.

Real estate developer, builder, operator.

Architect.

Fourth House Matters

Home (hotel, motel, apartment, house, hut, igloo, lodge, cottage, bungalow, trailer, houseboat, flat, castle, palace, chateau . . . the place where one lives, resides, dwells, lodges).

Real property one owns (lot, store, farm, cottage, motel, hotel, house, co-op apartment, condominium, building, shopping center, office, arcade, mausoleum, shopping mall or plaza).

Anything done to the home or real property, such as adding on, enlarging, extending, repairing, improving.

Gardens (cultivation of fruits, flowers, vegetables, herbs, trees).

Landscaping.

Domestic concerns and interests.

Business projects, undertakings and/or work performed from the home.

Mines (excavation, digging up ores and metals from the earth).

Conditions in one's closing days.

End of any matter . . . the termination or conclusion of any un-named event, fact or object.

Fifth House

Fifth House People

Children (one's own or another's).

Creativity.

Stockbroker.

Gambler (one who takes chances and speculates in business, the stock market, games of chance or anything where a gamble is involved).

Entertainers (movie, theatre, night club, circus, outdoor arena).

Sportsman, sportswoman.

Stunt man, stunt woman.

Lovers (beau, fiancé, sweetheart, romantic boyfriend or girl-friend).

Fifth House Matters

Hazards and the risks encountered in business or any venture.

Speculation (taking a chance, purchasing stock or other items for future sale at a higher price than one originally paid).

Wildcatting.

Games of chance (raffles, bingo, lotteries, roulette, dice, cards, slot machines, cockfights, racing . . . horse, greyhound, car).

Games (board games, charades).

Amusement and amusement places (arcades, concessions, movie theatres, operas, fairs, expositions).

Sporting events and places they are held (stadiums, arenas, under the circus tent, rodeos, bullfight rings).

Adventures that are perilous, chancy, risky, dangerous, daring and venturesome (skydiving, hand gliding, riding in a barrel over Niagara Falls, trick riding of cars and motorcycles, being shot out of a cannon, walking on fire).

Entertainment (entertaining or being entertained, parties, movies, theatre).

Show business.

Hobbies.

The pleasurable and fun areas of life . . . how one has fun.

Creativity (perform, put into effect, convey, enforce, carry out, demonstrate, exhibit, verbalize, vocalize and/or describe with imagination, inventiveness and originality).

Courtship (dates, spooning, wooing, serenading).

Love-making (romance, affection, necking, petting, liaison, sex).

One's attitude toward the sex act.

Companionship of children and/or those met in pleasant surroundings.

Childbirth.

Educational institutions (location where education is dispensed .
. . day and night school, nursery, grammar, grade, elemen-
tary, junior high and high school, preparatory).

Sixth House

Sixth House People

Employee (wage earner, laborer, crew, staff).

Subordinate (junior, lesser, lower and smaller rank than one).

Doorman.

Janitor, maintenance personnel.

Public and civil workers.

Personal and/or public servants.

One who gives service to others and waits upon others (maid,
governess, attendant).

One who works in medicine and/or with people who are ill (doctor, nurse, intern, physiotherapist).

Dietician, nutritionist.

Veterinarian.

One who works in a bar (bartender, waiter), restaurant (waiter,
busboy, carhop), drug store (pharmacist), store (as a clerk).

Fellow worker, coworker, team worker, associate.

Tenant (renter, lease-holder, occupant or inhabitant who pays for
residing in another's property).

Armed services (army, navy, air force).

Sixth House Matters

Working atmosphere, surroundings, quarters, office . . . the area
where one composes, creates, labors, toils or does business.

Conditions encountered while performing one's job . . . machinery, equipment, office materials and supplies.

How one performs a chore, task, post, job, work.

Any business requiring service to others.

The aid, assistance, help and service one gives or receives from others.

The attitudes of those one works with or employs . . . as well as one's attitude toward those one works with or employs.

Places where food is prepared and served (café, cafeteria, coffee shop, diner, drive-in, restaurant, food stand.

Food, diet, and nutrition.

Sickness and medical matters.

Small animals and pets (cats, dogs, birds, gerbils).

Seventh House

Seventh House People

Mate, spouse, husband, wife.

Business partner (co-owner, colleague, and associate who is in a trade enterprise with another, and by which each shares in some fixed proportion in profits and losses).

Sponsor (one who vouches for someone or something and stands back of it . . . co-signer on loans, notes).

Personal and theatrical managers.

Client (customer, purchaser, patron, buyer, protege).

Patient (a sick person under one's care).

The people met in public (one comes face to face with, is introduced to, encounters or confronts).

Stranger (outsider, unknown).

Competitor (opponent, rival, opposition).

Public and known enemies (one recognizes, realizes and is conscious of one's foes and adversaries).

The plaintiff (the party that institutes a suit in court).

The defendant (a person against whom an action is brought).

Seventh House Matters

Marriage, matrimony, wedlock, the married state, nuptial.

One's attitude toward the marriage partner.

Business partnerships.

One's attitude toward the business partner.

Law suits, legal actions, arraignments, impeachments, litigations, proceedings, indictments, summons, subpoenas, citations, writs.

War.

Contests (competition, match, tournament—the competitive part).

The attitude, reaction and response one receives from the public.

Episodes and happenings while in public contact.

Gain or loss occurred through meeting the public, client, patient, competitor, open enemy, sponsor, partner.

Eighth House

Eighth House People

One whose work deals with insurance, medicare, pensions, Social Security, loans, mortgages, escrow, taxes or other people's money (accountant, bookkeeper, controller, purser, paymaster, cashier, teller, money broker, economist, financier, treasurer, stock market broker).

Pawnbroker (money-lender). Investor (one who puts in money and expects a profit from the investment).

Backer (one who furnishes financial backing to finance or support an endeavor . . . an "angel" on Broadway is someone who puts money into a show and expects a percentage back, or a theatrical personal manager who invests in an actor and expects a percentage of the actor's salary). Collection agent or anyone who collects debts.

Non-material, bodiless, spirits or entities (those who have died in the physical plane and now reside in a non-physical sphere).

Eighth House Matters

Money of others (backers, sponsors, clients, bosses, public, business and/or marriage partners).

Royalties received from books or songs.

Percentages or residuals received from radio or television commercials, magazine and billboard ads, movies or television shows . . . series or a show that is repeated.

Dividends received from investments made in the stock market. Interest paid or received from loans, retail credit installment buying, savings accounts . . . the money received in interest payments when a bank or insurance company invests in real estate.

Mortgages (a legal paper pledging property to cover a debt . . . pledged as security).

Money in escrow.

Loans (banking, finance company, personal).

Borrowing money.

The manner one pays back borrowed money.

Debts (obligations, liabilities).

Collecting debts.

How a business or marriage partner borrows, loans or spends money and pays the bills . . . goes into debt and one's attitude toward the other person regarding these matters.

Joint banking.

Alimony (paying and receiving).

Trust funds.

Funds of a business corporation or enterprise.

Fund raising (political or otherwise to raise funds for the needy, a cause, charity, research).

Tax-exempt foundations involved in research or humanitarian endeavors.

Taxes (income, federal, state, city, local, sales, gift, property).

Pensions (subsidy, support, payment, allowance paid for past services after retirement).

Social Security.

Unemployment insurance.

Insurance (guarantee, warranty, premiums paid to build up funds
for compensation for death, loss or disability, or insurance
which works like a savings account).

Medicare.

Grants, scholarships, fellowships.

Gifts (presents, donations).

Bequests (wills or items handed down to descendants or others).

Inheritance.

Death.

The influence of those who have died in the physical (and now
reside in a non-physical sphere) upon those who are living in
the physical realm of existence.

Ninth House

Ninth House People

Teacher, instructor, master, tutor, coach, trainer, professor, educator . . . online, on radio or television, via DVD/CD, in a
school or other location.

Lecturer.

Newscaster.

Television or radio performer who appears and his or her voice
goes out over the air waves (announcer, actor, etc.).

Preacher (priest, minister, evangelist, pastor, parson, clergyman,
rabbi, revivalist, cardinal, pope).

Metaphysician (one who is versed in mental philosophy, dealing
with nature and causes of being and knowing).

Philosopher.

Published writer (author, free-lance writer, essayist, novelist,
poet, fiction writer, song writer, critic, reviewer, columnist)
who receives a byline in a column, newspaper, magazine article, on a book or on a song).

One who works in advertising, publishing, importing and/or exporting or deals with foreign countries.

Travel agencies.

Airline flight attendant, pilot, flyer, aviator, astronaut (one who travels long distances or to foreign countries . . . the distance which is long depends upon the individual's experience with travel).

Ambassador (diplomat, consul, envoy, emissary).

Lawyer (attorney, counselor-at-law).

Judge (justice of the peace, magistrate, chancellor . . . the ninth house is the court room, the tenth house is the position of authority).

Jury.

In-laws.

One involved in transmitting cables.

Ninth House Matters

Instructing, teaching, educating, tutoring, schooling.

Higher learning and thinking (colleges, universities, adult classes, vocational trade schools, schools of art, commercial, business, conservatory, astrology, metaphysical, occultism, spiritualism, psychic development, religious and Sunday schools).

Religion.

Philosophy.

Lecturing (a speech, address, sermon, a formal discourse on a set subject).

The public platform (soap box) where one expresses one's beliefs, opinions and thoughts.

Publicly expressed ideas, views, concepts, convictions, creeds, faith.

Broadcasting (all forms . . . radio, television, cable TV).

Advertising.

Publishing.

Published writing (article, book, play, song, etc.).

Long distance and/or foreign travel (trips, jaunts, journeys, tours, voyages, cruises or safaris to alien, remote or strange places).

Foreign affairs (concerns, interests, work, business, project, undertaking).

Foreign trade (swap, barter, exchange, purchase).

Foreign negotiations, transactions, dealings and international
traffic.

Importing (merchandise brought into a country from abroad).

Exporting (that which is sent out of a country).

United Nations business affairs, meetings and representatives of
countries expressing the countries beliefs, views and ideas . .
. world court.

International law.

Legal action (the court's verdict, ruling, decree, finding).

Cables (telegraphs, telegrams, wires).

Tenth House

Tenth House People

Mother (also foster or step-mother or grandmother).

In high rank or above one in station . . . one who controls others
because of his or her high position, power, authority, prestige, influence.

Administrators, directors, leaders, managers, chairman (modera-
tors, master of ceremonies), chairman of the board.

King, queen, emperor, president, premier, ruler, commander,
principal, headmaster . . . one who presides over an organization or republic.

Politician.

Governor.

Mayor.

Judges and popes (the authoritative position held).

Dignitaries.

Noted, renowned and famous celebrities.

Heroes and heroines.

VIPs.

Well known in the public eye or within the circle in which one
moves, trades or is in business.

Notorious and scandalous (known publicly in an unfavorable
way).

One who works in publicity . . . publicist, press agent, huckster,
ballyhooer.

Tenth House Matters

One's career, field, job, occupation, profession, vocation.

One's business accountability, reliability, burden, responsibility.

One's success or failure in business . . . one's attitude that attracts success or detracts from success.

One's classification, position, echelon, rank, status, spot.

One's influence, sway and power springing from one's position,
office, rank or station.

The ability to secure favors, holdings, prestige, authority, control.

The public attitude . . . what others think of one.

Public acknowledgment, homage, honor, respect.

Awards, prizes, trophies, honors, scholarships, diplomas, grants,
credits, distinctions, subsidies, titles and tokens for recognition and merit.

Reputation, public image.

Public Relations (one's name before the public by some channel
receiving publicity).

Publicity stunts.

Receiving fame by one's profession, publicity, notoriety.

Scandals (rumor, talk, gossip, dishonor, disgrace, notoriety to
one's name, public image. which effects the reputation).

Eleventh House

Eleventh House People

Acquaintance, comrade, chum, buddy, friend, confident, companion, crony, pal, classmate, playmate, roommate.

Eleventh House Matters

Type of friends and acquaintances one attracts.

The benefit (gain, profit, advantage, good, value) brought to one by one's friends and acquaintances.

The loss, disadvantage, bad or disapproval, criticism, fault-finding or problems that friends or acquaintances may bring to one.

How one's life is affected by acquaintances and friends.

Twelfth House

Twelfth House People

One who works behind the scenes (detective, policeman or policewoman, secret service, spy, secret, foreign or undercover agent, investigator, criminal, scientist, researcher, inventor, office worker who is hidden behind the scenes and does not talk with the public).

A non-professional spy.

One who works alone (writer).

One who deals with the confidential matters of others (astrologer, psychologist, counselor).

One who works in white or black magic.

One who works in witchcraft, spiritualism, psychic phenomena.

Magician (on stage, night clubs, movies, TV . . . the unknown factor of how one performs the magic tricks—secretly and mysteriously).

One who works in laboratories or in places of confinement, detention and/or restriction (asylums, sanitariums, hospitals, clinics, institutions, jails, prisons . . . doctor, nurse, intern, orderly, vet; warden, matron, guard).

Nurse in private practice.

One whose work deals with charity, relief, welfare, donation.

One who works with large livestock.

One who lives in a convent, monastery, concentration camp, isolation ward, sanitarium, hospital or home for the aged or mentally ill.

One who is in bondage to another.

Suicide victims or one who inflicts self-injury or self-destruction.

Hermits, recluses.

Secret enemies.

Twelfth House Matters

Silent, quiet and hushed concerns, deals, affairs, interests, business, work, projects, undertakings.

Private and secret negotiations.

Activities that one hides or knowledge that one keeps from others.

Covered, cached or hidden objects.

Out of the limelight (without focus, attention, spotlight, fame, publicity).

Living a cloistered life in a convent, monastery, deserted place, seclusion, isolation, privacy, shut-in alone, solitude, apart from others, camping away from others, retreating and withdrawing from people. These are actions of one's own doing.

Places of restriction, confinement, detainment, detention, imprisonment . . . to incarcerate, jail, put in a cage.

Concentration camps.

Being sent to Siberia (people sent there may escape and seek asylum in another country).

Asylums (places offering protection, safety, a refuge . . . for those in exile, the mentally ill or aged).

Isolation ward (a room, section or wing where a person is segregated, quarantined, secluded and kept apart from others).

Institutions (to work in one, to be committed to one or to be confined within the walls of one).

Homes for the aged where one is confined away from people and regulated to restrictions, rules; nursing homes.

Sanitariums (rest home, health retreat . . . where people are confined or bed-ridden).

Hospitals, clinics, rehabilitation facilities.

Work where one gives aid, assistance, relief.

Welfare work (organized to better the living conditions of the poor).

Charity work.

Benefits (any public entertainment of which the proceeds are pledged to charity).

Donations (private or anonymous contributions to charity).

Laboratories (of scientists, researchers, inventors, crime detection or anyone's private lab).

Research work (exploration, inquiry, investigation).

Detective, spy and secretive work (for government or private use).

Crime discovery.

Crime.

Felony.

Misdemeanor, misdeed, illegal actions.

Concealed, unrevealed and underhanded schemes, plans, contracts, meetings, arrangements, intrigues, maneuvers, routines, tasks, techniques.

Hideaway (hiding place, hideout for concealment, secret place, sanctum).

Rendezvous (a meeting place agreed upon in advance).

A mystery (unapprehended, unexplained and unascertained elements, factors, components or constituents . . . anything that is not known or its identity cannot be established or mystery revealed; for example, Amelia Earhart's and Adolf Hitler's disappearance-death . . . the actual and factual end result is unknown).

Black and white magic, witchcraft, voodoo, sorcery, wizardry, or magic performed by an entertainer (the mystery element).

Psychic phenomena.

Spiritualism.

Occultism.

Secret alliances.

Secret societies (Ku Klux Klan).

Secret orders (Eastern Star, Freemasons, The Benevolent and Protective Order of the Elks, etc.).

Spiritual retreats or retreats for psychic development, meditation, etc.

One's ability to keep a secret or confidence.

Secrets.

Confidential Affairs.

Limitations.

Sorrow (grief, woe, sadness, remorse, repentance, regret, disgruntlements, letdowns, disappointments).

Suicide (to destroy oneself or to take one's life).

Self-harm.

Self-injury.

To offend, wound or ruin oneself.

Large live stock, cattle, animals.

Chapter Two

The Aspects

One of the factors analyzed in reading a horoscope refers to the ten aspects made by the planets, Midheaven (MC) and Ascendant (Asc). The aspects fall into three categories. *Harmonious:* Trine, sextile and semisextile. *Discordant:* Opposition, square, semi-square and sesquisquare. *Neutral:* Conjunction, inconjunct and parallel. Refer to the diagram in the front of this book for the symbol of each of these aspects.

Semisextile

Harmonious Aspect   Key: Small Chances

One attracts small chances that are not evident. Once noticed or offered, press ahead because one must goad these small chances into action if they are to be worthwhile. Slight increases can be produced but the results may take time. Meanwhile the experience gained can be helpful and valuable.

Sextile

Harmonious Aspect   Key: Big Chances

One attracts big chances. Seize whatever is presented. Employ action, buckle down to hard work and devote productive energy to everything. Aim high for all of the benefits. The doors to many avenues may open if these advantageous chances are utilized. Otherwise, once they have passed, they are gone and cannot be recalled.

Trine

Harmonious Aspect   Key: Good Fortune

One is favored, protected and attracts good fortune, a windfall, success. These things come freely and minus too much toil or exertion. Prosperity can result; therefore, one should seize all of the "goodies" presented on the golden platter.

Semisquare

Discordant Aspect   Key: Annoyances

One feels peeved, riled, provoked and attracts unimportant annoyances, aggravations, nuisances, irritations, displeasures, disapprovals, fault-findings or unfavorable comments. Shifts of scene, alteration, change and deviation may take place. These events may bring doubt, apprehension, indecision, irresolution or disbelief. One allows small disharmonies to amass into larger ones. As they increase to a substantial size, the sparks begin to fly.

To benefit: Rise above them by ignoring them and dismissing them from one's thoughts. Use the energy as a tool by channeling these feelings into constructive endeavors.

Sesquisquare

Discordant Aspect   Key: Disturbances

Disturbances, commotions, jolts, shocks and excitement reign. Current and prevailing situations can be unexpectedly rendered asunder. These upheavals may make one feel flurried, in a frenzy and all shook-up. One moment the thoughts may be agreeable and nice. At the next moment the thoughts may be disagreeable and displeasing. Mind and body disturbances may result.

To benefit: Utilize this energy by diversifying it in a dissimilar course. Willingly receive whatever comes because new doors may open bringing better conditions.

Square

Discordant Aspect   Key: Barrier

There are several kinds of wishes that one sets one's heart on. These desires and aspirations are represented by the planets involved in the aspect and the houses that the planets rule. Barriers, hindrances and blockages to these desires are placed in one's pathway because of how one behaves (discordant side of planets and the following courses of action) and relates to the areas of life (houses) involved in the aspect.

One may attract extreme and stormy dissensions and disagreements which cause strain, stress and a battle. Unrestrained, one may be careless, reckless, heedless, coarse, rude, impetuous, loud and erupt by blowing one's stack (top). This course of action could wreck and ruin all that one touches or contacts.

To benefit: All barriers, hindrances and problems should be met with a happy attitude. Think of them as a measure to test one's endurance. Control and master all discordant feelings and actions. When they have been conquered and defeated, feel elated that the victory over them was won by using effort in constructive channels.

Opposition

Discordant Aspect   Key: Conflicts

An emotional and mental seesaw effect. The thoughts are simultaneously torn back and forth between two highly desirable things. Conflicts are attracted because one wants both things equally. With the opposition one cannot have one's cake and eat it too, nor can one travel in two directions at the same time. It is necessary to select one desire and to give up the other. This forfeiture causes a parting and breaking between the two different sets of desires.

To benefit: Analyze, weigh and carefully examine all the pros and cons involved in the decision to be made. When making a choice, one should maintain a positive outlook and be sure that there is not too much emotion, feeling or sentiment entering into the decision. Progress is made when decisions are made, which thus makes this aspect a necessary one.

Inconjunct

Neutral Aspect   Key: Inflated-Deflated

This aspect indicates inflated thoughts, usually with deflated results. One attracts situations to expand, but nothing much results. Things are driven asunder rather than in unison. One moment one expects an increase, the next moment one expects a decrease. The feelings are sort of "blah" . . . one is not in a happy frame of mind, nor an unhappy frame of mind. This aspect is similar to a balloon one inflates, only to watch it deflate. Nothing comes of the ideas represented by the planets involved unless the energy is directed.

The inconjunct aspect becomes harmonious when involved with Venus or Jupiter *unless* Venus or Jupiter is in an aspect with Mars or Saturn. In the former case the chances attracted require energy, action and power for a beneficial usage. One must refine, improve and work on everything attracted. In the latter case the aspect is neutral.*

The inconjunct aspect becomes discordant when involved with Mars or Saturn *unless* Mars or Saturn is in an aspect with Venus or Jupiter. In the former case the barriers and hindrances are not too laborious or rough to rise above or overcome. The disharmony involved can be transformed into an advantage. In the latter case the aspect is neutral.*

Parallel

Neutral Aspect   Key: Intensified Action and Thought

Uncertain and obscure desires are gradually developed and built up with greater strength, force and power with each passing day, month or year. This is dependent upon the length of time the aspect is in orb.

After some time the feelings and thoughts are enhanced and intensified to such a degree that conditions and events are attracted relating to the planets and houses involved in the aspect.

The parallel aspect becomes harmonious when involved with Venus or Jupiter *unless* Mars or Saturn is in an aspect with Venus or Jupiter. In the former case the aspect can be more auspicious. In the latter case the aspect is neutral.*

The parallel aspect becomes discordant when involved with Mars or Saturn *unless* Mars or Saturn is in an aspect with Venus or Jupiter. In the former case the aspect can be more inauspicious. In the latter case the aspect is neutral.*

If a parallel aspect is added to another aspect, the aspect already there is enhanced and intensified to a greater degree than the aspect would express by itself. For example, a Trine with a parallel would be heightened and have more strength to bring good fortune . . . intensified good fortune.

Conjunction

Neutral Aspect   Key: Conspicuous, Noticeable

The matters and traits ruled by the planets and houses involved in the aspect are conspicuous and stand out for everyone to notice. Attention is attracted because of the power, force and energy used in expressing these traits and actions. The spotlight is on one's abilities and talents. The conjunction aspect brings *more of*, and an *overdoing of*, the traits and matters listed under the planets' meanings. These traits are drawn out and highlighted . . . everything is overemphasized and stressed.

A conjunction aspect becomes harmonious when involved with Venus or Jupiter *unless* Venus or Jupiter is in an aspect with Mars or Saturn. In the former case the aspect can be pleasing and agreeable. In the latter case the aspect is neutral.*

A conjunction aspect becomes discordant when involved with Mars or Saturn *unless* Mars or Saturn is in an aspect with Venus or Jupiter. In the former case the aspect can be unpleasant and disagreeable. In the latter case the aspect is neutral.*

The good or bad attracted is the consequence of one's own doing rather than outside forces.

Following is how to tell whether a neutral planet involved in the neutral conjunction aspect will work harmoniously or discordantly:

Look at *all* of the other aspects the two planets (involved in the aspect) are making to the other planets in the chart. It is the sum total of harmony or discord that will give a clue as to how the person is using the energy.

For example, consider a chart with the Sun and Mercury (both neutral) in a conjunction aspect. The Sun and Mercury both have more discordant aspects than harmonious ones. Therefore, the individual is more likely to use the energy in a discordant manner. By major progression, if both the Sun and Mercury are afflicted during the same time period, it is probable that the conjunction aspect would work discordantly. By major progression, if both the Sun and Mercury are making mostly harmonious aspects during the same time period, it is possible for the aspect (conjunction) to work harmoniously.

Note: All aspects represent energy. The nature of their expression depends upon how one uses the energy.

---

*To gain a better understanding of neutral aspects, see *How To Read Cosmodynes* by Doris Chase Doane, American Federation of Astrologers, 2009.

Chapter Three

The Planets

One of the factors in delineating the horoscope refers to the ten planets. The Sun and Moon are luminaries, but for convenience, astrologers call them planets. The following descriptions embrace both the higher and lower expression of each planet's energy. The planetary symbols can be found on the diagram in the front of this book.

Harmonious Sun

One Who . . .
Does things with all of his might.
Uses his influence to have his way.
Knows his own mind.
Holds his own ground.
Carries authority.
Takes or assumes command.
Dominates conditions.
Guides others.

One Who Is . . .
Dependable, solid as a rock, unyielding, stable, staunch, a tower
  of strength, a powerhouse, power-driven.

In a top position or at the head of an enterprise, a business, undertaking or venture.

Great in a field of endeavor, renowned, well-known, reputable,
respected by others, celebrated, illustrious, honored, famed,
in the limelight, distinguished, dignified, stately, regal, of
royal blood or married to royalty, proud, certain, kind.

One Who Desires . . .

Approval, acceptance, having everyone under his control, su-
premacy.

Self-esteem, self-respect.

Leadership, rulership, prominence, recognition, prestige, distinctions.

Winning votes, elections or honors.

Receiving titles, advancements or upgrades in position or rank.

To be great or the best in whatever he undertakes, to be some-
body and make a splash.

One Who Can . . .

Direct his aims, ambitions and wishes.

Make decisions.

Stick to his guns; remain firm; stand fast.

Oversee or supervise others; require others to do as he suggests;
rule, control, direct, administer or reign over others; bestow,
award or concede privileges to others.

Gain recognition, shine, glow.

One Who Has . . .

Vigor, verve, vivacity, endurance, virility, get up and go.

Self-control, self-mastery, self-command, a will or mind of his
own.

Determination, strength of purpose, energy, force, strength.

A hold over others, the inside track, power (proves it by pulling
strings), jurisdiction over others, the driver's seat, others at
his beck and call.

The aptitude, competence and flair to command, lead and instruct others; executive ability.

Prestige, a title (royal or in an office, company, organization, club).

One May Attract . . .

An award, honorable mention or a prize, trophy, gold star, citation, medal, decoration of honor, scholarship, diploma, fellowship, doctorate, degree, promotion, title (with a company or royal), grant, subsidy or receive credit for one's actions or ideas.

An interest in politics.

A desire to go into business for oneself.

Type of People . . .

One who uses the actions and traits listed under the harmonious side of the Sun, or whose hobby and/or work deals with anything listed under the harmonious side of the Sun.

Employer, taskmaster, executive, administrator, controller, supervisor, superintendent, chief.

Business person, industrialist, impresario, entrepreneur.

Office holder, officer, authority figure.

Judge.

Federal or government official.

Chairman or chairwoman.

Politician, mayor, governor, diplomat, ambassador, dignitary, premier, prime minister, president, ruler, king, queen.

Connoisseur, expert.

Winner, hero, heroine.

Director, producer, headliner, star.

The masculine sex (boys, males, men, gentlemen).

One Whose Hobby and/or Work Deals With . . .

Anything listed under the harmonious side of the Sun, gold, securities, solar energy.

Discordant Sun

Note: The actions and traits that follow are mainly perpetrated because of egoism.

One Who . . .

Will do almost anything to gain attention, recognition or to impress others.

Flaunts importance for all to notice, name-drops, struts, brags, boasts, blows one's own horn, holds one's nose in the air, lords it over others, tramples and rides over others, orders and dominates others in a depreciating or derogatory way, gives orders in a bossy manner, controls others.

Makes or sets the rules, ordinances.

Commands and drives his authority in a manner that makes others aware of him or impresses them.

Reigns, governs, rules the roost, decrees, instructs, prescribes, manipulates.

Perpetrates and does unsocial and hostile actions, deeds, undertakings or work.

Affects, influences, moves and inspires other people in an egotistical manner.

One Who Is . . .

Arrogant, a stuffed shirt, a snob, a bloated aristocrat, high and mighty, lofty, assuming, smug, aloof.

Presumptuous, magisterial, imperious, authoritative, insistent, demanding, bigoted, intolerant, pretentious, haughty, power happy.

Vain, showy, a grand-stander, an exhibitionist.

Self-seeking, self-centered (ego trip).

Disrespectful, unyielding, stubborn.

An eager beaver, excessively aspiring and zealous.

One Who Desires . . .

And adores approval and acceptance by the hand clapping, cheer or praise of others.

Acknowledgments, acclaim, all of the glory or credit.

Prominence and to be distinguished, important, notable, indispensable and featured over others.

To be a star or headliner and receive top billing.

To be a hero or heroine.

To hold the spotlight in one's own circle and go out of the way to be in the limelight . . . this is done in a manner that makes others realize that the person doing it has an ego problem.

To be the master, controller, director, leader or boss of others.

Esteem, regard, respect, honors, awards, degrees, trophies, medals or prizes so he can shine and show-off.

Publicity.

A job, post or status with weight, control, distinction, eminence.

Wealth so one can have the upper hand.

To go into business for oneself.

One's own techniques, procedures.

To be the master, expert, connoisseur because one wants to be better and greater than others.

One Who Has . . .

Self-praise, self-regard, a good opinion of self, self-respect, self-satisfaction, self-esteem.

An excessive, unreasonable or untrue immodesty, self-esteem.

A feeling of being superior to others . . . feels that he is above others and beyond reproach.

A godly attitude toward others.

A domineering or overbearing disposition, outlook, air, bearing or carriage.

A lack of sympathy for what other people are entitled to, deserve, merit, earn or are worthy of because he wants these things for self.

An inferiority complex (also Saturn) . . . feels he does not measure up to, or falls short of, standards he sets for self . . . self-disapproval sets in and he may make up for his lack of confidence by appearing conceited and bragging; a feeling of embarrassment or disgrace.

One May Attract Difficulties With . . .

The masculine sex.

A person in a higher position than one.

Attaining an advancement, a higher position, a raise or an award, honor or a diploma, prize.

Trying to receive recognition, praise or credit . . . others may block one's efforts or attempt to hold one back or down.

The alienation of those in upper rank because one has trouble getting along with others because of an ego attitude . . . others are not impressed by the actions and traits used (listed under Sun discordant).

There Is Less of the Following . . .

Liveliness, vivacity, endurance, energy, stamina, virility or strength. This is dependent upon the other active aspects by major progression. In many cases the discordant side of the Sun gives one more energy but the person may become exhausted faster.

Type of People . . .

One who uses the actions and traits listed under the harmonious side of the Sun negatively and/or one who uses the traits listed under the discordant side of the Sun. Also one whose hobby and/or work deals with anything listed under the harmonious or discordant side of the Sun.

One Whose Hobby and/or Work Deals With . . .

Anything listed under the harmonious or discordant side of the Sun.

Harmonious Moon

One Who ...

Requires, wants or must have a change, diversity, contrast, alteration or deviation from the normal everyday routine, of life.

Needs variety.

Feels his home life is important, enjoys domestic chores . . . cooking, sewing.

Becomes involved with the female sex for personal or business purposes.

Interviews others.

Makes an imprint upon the public or another.

One Who Is ...

Being interviewed.

Interested in music (from the feeling angle).

Constantly changing, shifting, wavering, unfixed, unstable, undecided.

Always altering, revising and amending his style, manner or state of mind.

Off and on with the emotions, feelings, moods.

Capricious, restless (due to a mood), many-sided, flexible, bending, adaptable, open-minded.

Receiving, suggestible, susceptible, easily influenced, impressionable, sensitive, instinctive, intuitive (from a feeling or hunch).

Accommodating.

Inquisitive, searching.

In harmony with others, popular, liked by many people.

Weak, powerless, lacking strength or power.

Home-loving, a stay-at-home, a homebody, domesticated, housebroken.

One Who Desires ...

Variety.

To be the protector of the family.

To watch over, shelter or to take care of others by being maternal or paternal.

To nurse those who are handicapped, ill or without strength.

To take animals under one's wing and tend to them.

One Who Can ...

Comprehend, grasp and understand other people's problems, likes or dislikes.

Change and shift with the wind.

Change the moods with the tides.

Imitate others by using one's emotions and feelings, thereby creating a mood and feeling so as to appear to be the person he is imitating.

Mimic, mock or ape others.

Inquire, request, appeal and apply for favors, kindness, good will, support, help, benefits and assistance and, in turn, receive them.

Beneficially and profitably buy or sell in large quantities or at a lesser price (due to volume buying the price is cheaper and one can therefore afford to sell in volume).

One Who Has ...

Fans rooting for and applauding, and others standing behind him and cheering him on.

Mental and emotional receptivity.

Clairvoyance, supernatural and telepathic experiences, ordeals, events and occurrences.

One May Attract ...

Extensive, far-reaching and favorable publicity.

Ordinary, mediocre or hum-drum talk; chit-chat; tete-a-tete; informal or familiar talk.

Favorable interviews or interrogations.

Highlights in or to the home.

Everyday, common and habitual personal or business affairs.

A change or improvement in one's emotional disposition or outlook, a change of moods, more subconscious thinking and reacting than what is normally used.

Type of People ...

One who uses the actions and traits listed under the harmonious side of the Moon, or whose hobby and/or work deals with anything listed under the harmonious side of the Moon. The usual, average, common, plain, ordinary, mediocre type of people that make up a category, denomination, group or section.

Fans, followers, devotees.

Nurse, waiter, waitress, cook, nutritionist, housewife, seamstress, maid, store clerk, musician, the feminine sex (girls, females, women, ladies).

One Whose Hobby and/or Work Deals With ...

Anything listed under the harmonious side of the Moon.

Meeting and contacting the common populace and/or employed in catering to and waiting upon others through daily contact.

The home, homemade things (items), housekeeping, cooking, sewing, nursing.

Food, food industry, broker, grocery stores.

Feminine items.

Retail trade.

Vending and marketing in mass, bulk or large quantities.

Women.

Personnel (interviewing, casting, etc.).

Music.

Discordant Moon

One Who . . .

Fluctuates back and forth trying to make up his mind (from an emotional standpoint).

Depends upon whims of the moment, oscillates

Becomes uninterested, weary, tired, blase or unconcerned about events or people.

Stops, ceases, leaves, abandons, deserts and gives up in mid-course on work, affairs, aims, intentions, undertakings or business.

Does things half-way and fails to finish, complete or see things to an end.

Lacks determination.

Tells rumors, draws unfavorable publicity, feels mentally dull.

One Who Is . . .

Endlessly and interminably changing, deviating or altering feelings, thoughts or actions.

Indecisive, uncertain, emotionally or subconsciously confused, baffled, mixed up, jumbled, disoriented, befuddled.

Many-sided, inconsistent, fickle and changeable.

Frivolous, subject to change, unsettled, roving, difficult and tough to hold down, unstable, unsteady, unreliable due to emotions or moods, weak-kneed, bored, discontented, displeased, flippant, frustrated, unpopular, a wallflower (too sensitive, feeling that others will not like him; therefore, he wants to be left out . . . afraid of getting his feelings hurt).

Too demonstrative, responsive, impressionable, susceptible and touchy with people in an over-emotional manner.

One Who Desires . . .

Variety.

To wander, stroll or rove here and there.

One Who Has . . .

Inconveniences, predicaments and troubles with the average, common classes of people, or with females.

Daily and frequent habits, business, undertakings, interests and functions prove to be a source of difficulty.

His moods turned upside down.

A problem with bringing any mental application to the center of the thoughts.

A clash, disharmony or disagreement with one's feelings, sentiments and sensibilities.

Psychosomatic illnesses (physical symptom attributed to a person's emotional condition).

A disposition or outlook of living for the moment and for tomorrow.

A mood to get lost, vanish or go astray to wheresoever the whim takes him.

Emotions that run at a high tide.

The lesser, unimportant trivial matters taking too much emotional attention, resulting in an emotional tizzy.

Family, domestic or home conditions that are topsy-turvy or changes occur in the home.

Problems where there is pain and suffering (mental, which leads to emotional upsets).

One May Attract . . .

Difficulties with women.

Family upsets.

Unwise or aimless moves or changes.

Unlikable, distasteful, unacceptable and uncomfortable ordeals and tribulations.

Desires that may be ungratified, foiled or thwarted.

Disadvantageous and adverse talk, rumor, idle tales, gossip and tattling (either one does it to others, or others do it to one).

Unpopularity and being less liked by people.

Type of People . . .

One who uses the actions and traits listed under the harmonious
    side of the Moon negatively and/or one who uses the actions
    and traits listed under the discordant side of the Moon. Also
    one whose hobby and/or work deals with anything listed un-
    der the harmonious or discordant side of the Moon.

One Whose Hobby and/or Work Deals With . . .

Anything listed under the harmonious or discordant side of the
    Moon.

Harmonious Mercury

Note: Mercury aspects indicate a way of communicating . . .
that way is dependent upon the other planet in the aspect. The
meaning of the other planet explains how one communicates.

One Who . . .

Communicates his outlook to others, gives the facts, gives an ac-
    count, notifies others, serves a notice to others, keeps others
    posted, keeps abreast of the times.

Brings others or items up to date.

Keeps tabs, keeps an eye on or checks on people or things.

Knows the answers, the score, the ropes and all of the ins and
    outs.

Overhears conversations.

Receives reliable messages.

Brings, sends or leaves word.

Gives a word to the wise.

Gives good tidings.

Receives the news, scoop, reports, statements, notifications.

Knows things that are newsworthy.

Views things in a new light.

Looks back upon things (events).

Uses common sense.

Watches the clock . . . is aware of time . . . and on time rather than late.

Questions others for a reason or explanation.

Uses well-defined or distinct and impartial, unbiased and unprejudiced thoughts or reasoning.

Learns (acquires) knowledge.

Thinks hard, racks one's brains, puzzles over things.

Unscrambles, unravels, untangles, deciphers, decodes or clears things; finds the answer or solution.

Teaches, tutors, grooms, coaches, trains, drills, gives exercises, lessons or instructions.

One Who Is . . .

Intelligently and intellectually sharp, acute, incisive and goes ahead making progress as he advances along.

Clear-headed, wide-awake, watchful and observant (also Saturn . . . Mercury is the mental and curious part), witty, attentive and quick-witted, brilliant, smart, astute, discerning, brainy, knowledgeable, sensible, aware of and appreciates a superior or higher background (with education), scholarly, thoughtful, meditative, searching, smart as a whip, quick on the trigger; nobody's fool, in the know, wise, well-read, well-versed, well-educated, a book-worm, an intellectual highbrow, a treasury of information

Preoccupied, engrossed and absorbed in thought.

Smartly or cleverly facetious, talkative, nosey, a tipster, an eyewitness.

Agile, spry, nimble, flexible, lithe, adept, skillful, mobile, many-sided, fluent, articulate, slick, smooth, suave.

An excellent, superb or worthy speaker, spokesperson, conversationalist, imitative (also the Moon . . . Mercury is the voice, words, speech, singing and talking part).

One Who Desires To . . .

Travel, take a jaunt or trip.

Obtain, gain, pick up, attain and add to, heighten, increase, expand and enlarge information, knowledge, know-how, experience, wisdom.

Listen to the news because he is interested in what is happening.

Browse.

Scan newspapers, magazines or books.

Think things over, revise thoughts.

One Who Can . . .

Make an important decision because good reasoning and logic goes into each thought.

Effectuate and decide significant, meaningful, serious, weighty and momentous determinations, conclusions, settlements, rulings, findings, judgments and verdicts.

Acknowledge, understand or see certain, sure, definite and reliable elements, components or constituent parts.

Comprehend and mentally grasp an inkling of subjects or factors.

Adjust, agree and reconcile matters rapidly, quickly and speedily resulting in a clear understanding by all.

Express oneself in the most desirable, useful and helpful manner by using serviceable and priceless ideas, concepts or theories; store knowledge.

Gather information.

Retain things because of a good memory, know things by heart, recall and remember things because of the acute mental faculties.

Be taught, be enlightened, fathom things better than others.

Discover the answer, explanation or outcome to problems.

Hit upon a solution.

Pump others for information and receive it victoriously.

Take oral or written examinations successfully.

One Who Has . . .

His eyes open.

A nose for the news and what is the talk of the town, or in the air, bandied about and circulated.

Information about people, occurrences or objects.

Good mental impressions, ripe ideas.

Facility for lengthy, protracted, complex, complicated and difficult formulas, techniques or methods.

A liberal education.

A realization.

An amusing and enjoyable manner of telling funny tales, accounts, yarns and episodes.

One May Attract . . .

A change for the better.

Shifting, alternating, revolving and varying conditions, predicaments, situations, circumstances.

Accepts new chores or endeavors easily, promptly and quickly because the aptitude, facility and capability to acquire knowledge and master that which is taught, or that which one is involved with, is at its peak.

Smaller odds or less chance of making blunders, errors, inaccuracies or mistakes.

Unfavorable comments or fault-finding that can be helpful.

Favorable chances to sign papers, deeds, contracts, documents, legal papers, or formal agreements.

Type of People . . .

One who uses the actions and traits listed under the harmonious side of Mercury, or whose hobby and/or work deals with anything listed under the harmonious side of Mercury.

Reporter, journalist, writer, columnist, reviewer, critic, commentator, news broadcaster, announcer, narrator, master or mistress of ceremonies, lecturer, linguist.

Comic, mimic (also the Moon; Mercury is the communication

part), impersonator (also Neptune; Mercury is the speech part), singer

Messenger, courier, dispatch bearer.

Transportation workers, cab drivers, chauffeurs.

Traveling salespeople (also Jupiter)

Traveler.

Librarian.

Teacher, tutor.

Clerical worker, secretary, stenographer, data entry, keyboard.

Accountant, bookkeeper, auditor.

Office, postal or telephone worker.

Switchboard operator.

Analyst, interpreter.

Lawyer.

Draftsman.

Distributor.

Agent (theatrical, ticket, travel, postal, railroad or bus . . . any type of broker or representative).

One Whose Hobby and/or Work Deals With . . .

Anything listed under the harmonious side of Mercury.

Jotting down, noting or writing outlines, contours, figurations.

Rapid, speedy and quick performance, movement, procedures and operations using reasoning and any thinking process.

Using or relying upon memory.

Audible, distinct and definite ways of phrasing, wording, delivering and accenting theories, thoughts, views, notions and concepts.

Addressing or appealing to others through conversing, chatting, discussing, consulting or advising.

Composition, transcription, correspondence, outlines, essays, drafts, excerpts, manuscripts, articles, novels, poetry, short stories, composing songs.

Any word, phrase, thought or idea said orally or composed on paper.

Mental labor; reviewing, utilizing, employing and applying the mental faculties; brain; intellectual activity.

Utilizing, practicing and adopting discreet or alert analysis, deductions, conclusions, thinking, logic.

Assiduous, studious, calculating or considered thinking.

Clarification and resolution of confusion, uncertainty, baffling things.

Intellect.

Straight thinking.

Finding results.

Examination of anything that determines its make-up; identifying things; investigation resolving and answering any matter which is a riddle, or which has an issue or a question to be answered.

Distinguishing, differentiating or sifting through objects or things.

Having detailed correctness, exactness and exclusion of error.

Having the mind in action or motion.

Informing; guiding; counseling.

Follows the laws and exact principles of science and concerns, subject matters and topics pertaining to science.

Maintaining, providing or sustaining notes, memorandums, journals, minutes, reports, registers, archives, logs, transcripts in a correct, orderly, categorical, even or direct manner.

Reckoning by numbers and computations, auditing.

Mathematics (also Mars), algebra, arithmetic, trigonometry

Sleep learning (also Neptune).

Translating, interpreting or learning languages.

Reading, studying, lecturing, singing, yodeling, chanting, crooning, serenading.

Ad-libbing, extemporizing or improvising (also Uranus).

Commuting, transportation.

Tours (also Pluto; Mercury is the information and travel part).

Communication, informing others of news (telegrams, bulletins, newsletters, news reports), intercoms.

Voice-overs (on radio or TV commercials, or phonograph recordings), dubbing the voice (in movies or animated cartoons).

Books, novels, albums, brochures, essays, manuals, handbooks, pocketbooks, hardcover books, textbooks, reference books, encyclopedias, dictionaries, almanacs, thesauruses, magazines, periodicals, newspapers, mails, email, text messages.

Discordant Mercury

One Who . . .

Lacks firmness, steadiness.

Changes, alters, varies, diversifies and switches concepts, ideas, views and notions too much.

Makes unfavorable comments about, or to others . . . or others do this to one.

Snitches, prattles, blabs, tells idle tales or dishes the dirt.

Annoys, nags or scolds others.

Constantly shifts speech or thoughts (a lack of continuity).

Talks too much, usually about nothing.

Gives or receives unreliable messages, dishonors and disgraces others.

One Who Is . . .

Easily moved or upset (mentally).

Gabby, chatty, nosey, excessively loquacious, garrulous, an informer, a chatterer, a tattler, a squealer, a stool-pigeon, a tattletale, a busybody, a meddler, a peddler or trader of gossip, long-winded.

A fault-finder, cutting, biting, caustic or too sharp with the speech or through the written word, overly disapproving, displeased and feels disgruntled with normal, accustomed and difficult matters which require a settlement or solution.

Bothered about idle rumors, tattling, scandal.

Too outspoken, unreserved with speech, crabby, cross, testy, a pest, uneasy, fidgety, nervous, fussy, fretful, sleepless, inconstant, late (not punctual), changeable, distracted, unsteady, shaky, giddy (also Neptune), high-strung, jumpy, can't sit still, moves from one chair to another, restless, paces.

Disorganized, untidy, unmanageable, unmethodical, mentally confused, hesitant, wavering, unfixed, unsettled, vacillating, indefinite.

Perplexed, stumped, puzzled, flustered, mixed-up, disoriented, rattled, many-sided.

Mentally misguided, misinterpreted, misconstrued, misunderstood, mistaken, quizzical, inattentive.

Contented, delighted, glad and enraptured when hearing bad news, tidings or rumors.

One Who Has . . .

His mind in disharmony, out of whack or not in smooth running order.

Mental ailments.

The mind too tense, mussed up and in confusion with pandemonium reigning.

Mental mix ups, mental uneasiness.

Unwise or ill-considered changes.

Mental dissension, mind tortured by problems.

Reasoning, thoughts or any mental effort repeated over and over again like a broken record.

The jitters, the willies.

Difficulty ending, completing, concluding and terminating intentions, aims, plans and undertakings.

Problems when uttering, discussing, showing, revealing, believing in or having faith in new ideas, notions, concepts, theories, impressions or surmises.

Impulsive opinions or presumptions.

Worthless, futile, inept or ineffectual talk, lecture or address with a timeless and unending stream, gushing or running of phrases, vocabulary, context, wording, ideas and conclusions that achieve or fulfill nothing.

Too many preoccupations.

So many things clogging the mind and making it difficult to render a decision, to think, reason or to talk coherently, impressions, notions and inklings that are in error, incorrect, inaccurate or mistaken.

Speech impediments (stammering, stuttering, lisping).

A task focusing or assembling anything of a mental nature.

Problems with committing things to memory or recalling the past.

Nervous mental tensions resulting in twitching, uncertainty, stage fright (Mercury the nervous part; Saturn the fear part), overly busy mind that is active and filled with a variety of ideas and thoughts which all work at the same time.

Problems and snags with paying attention, giving heed, mentally applying and bringing things to the center of the mind.

Ideas and speech flow in opposite directions or do not follow in order.

Unimportant, worthless, small, piddling annoyances and exasperations.

One Who Feels ...

Tense, uneasy, or jittery as if he is falling apart and becoming unhinged.

Nervous, fatigued due to the nerves being overtaxed.

Perturbed because bills arrive, are in error, or have not been paid.

Upset by bad news or messages received through the mail, telephone, email, text messaging or telegram.

Upset because of misreading or mistranslating written communication, book or article.

Shaken because of receiving or writing an improper or inappropriate letter, email or text message.

One May Attract . . .

Ridicule or be the one who ridicules.

Misunderstandings through speech or writing.

Mistakes, blunders, slip-ups, misprints, oversights, bloopers, boners, goofs, omissions, misapplications, or inaccuracies . . . one neglects to catch errors.

People who push one to the limit or test and try one's calm endurance; problems with phrasing, stating and saying things too fast, quickly, rushed or hurried; difficulty when writing important or serious letters or notes.

Problems when offering articles, essays, compositions, manuscripts or transcripts for publication, printing or editing; problems when signing, or because of signing papers, contracts, documents, deeds or deals (usually because one does not take the time to read the details, all that is written, or one may have trouble concentrating on the exact purport involved).

Type of People . . .

One who uses the actions and traits listed under the harmonious side of Mercury negatively and/or who uses the actions and traits listed under the discordant side of Mercury.

One whose hobby and/or work deals with anything listed under the harmonious or discordant side of Mercury.

One Whose Hobby and/or Work Deals With . . .

Anything listed under the harmonious or discordant side of Mercury.

Harmonious Venus

One Who . . .

Uses terms of endearment or intimacy.

Plays cupid.

Betters, enriches or cultivates through personal contact (social areas) the public, society or fashionable connections and affiliations; enjoys or thinks highly of the picturesque, adept or skillful in the fine arts.

Shows, presents, spreads and unveils excellent, admirable or first class items, objects, worthy breeding, courtesy and refinement.

Likes, prefers, desires and wishes others happiness and good health.

Seeks familiarity.

Approves, thinks highly of, values, realizes and has a sensitive understanding of color mixtures, fusions and blendings.

Plays and has fun.

Glows with beauty.

Attracts one's interest.

Appreciates anything or anyone that is pretty, lovely, graceful, elegant, exquisite, attractive, stunning or statuesque.

Becomes interested in the world of fashion; takes the easy way out; receives compliments.

One Who Is . . .

Fond of, delights in and relishes fun, amusements, luxuries or any agreeable emotions or recreations.

Free, easy, fun loving and seeks entertainment or pleasure; pleased as a child with a new toy.

Delighted by gifts, friendships, love.

Kind, genial, soft, tender, sweet, delightful, lovely, comely, winsome, engaging, pleasing, cheerful, entertaining, amusing, agreeable, appealing, fetching, friendly, affable, amiable, chummy, companionable, congenial, cordial, light-hearted, beaming, joyous, fun, frolicsome, mirthful, glad, pleasant, festive, lovable, close, demonstrative, warm-hearted, soft-hearted.

Emotional with the affections or infatuated, sensuous, moving, stirring, full of the most tender love feelings, in love, submissive, obedient with love, partly slavish and servile with the loved one, pliable, honeyed, luscious, melodious, forgiving, gracious, selfless, uncalculating, generous, giving.

Charming, personable, good looking, presentable, becoming, fair, beauteous, diverting, open-minded, interested in receiving others as a guest, socially prone, gregarious, liking social contacts.

Placid, quiet, restful, tranquil, undisturbed, romantic, aesthetic, graceful, cultured, tasteful, chic, refined, well-groomed, well-kept, tidy, orderly, scrupulous and careful in dress, delectable, delicate, exquisite, mild, moderate, polite, attentive, mannerly, genteel, well-behaved.

Stylish, sleek, dapper, dressy, nifty, in style, in vogue, in the height of fashion, debonaire, artistic.

Concerned with and takes notice of better, improved, preferable and superior objects, articles or finer things of life.

One Who Desires . . .

The plush things of life, costly items.

Picturesque scenery, painting, the beautiful, the pictorial.

To mingle with people, go to parties, be wined and dined or do the wining and dining.

Happy and fun-filled moments.

To visit a person or persons one is fond of.

Courtesy, compliments, to be kissed, affection.

One Who Can . . .

Receive, accept and welcome gifts from others in a gracious manner.

Enjoy life.

Please others and attract others in order to please them.

One Who Has . . .

A circle of acquaintances to socialize with.

A romance.

Feelings of fondness for another.

An interest in the affairs of others.

A love for peace and harmony.

An awareness or delicate perception of aesthetic qualities or values.

A desire for symmetry, beautiful shapes or forms.

Style, polish, winning ways.

An ardent and powerful wish to satisfy, delight and enchant another, a proposal, a request made of his emotions and sentiments.

The feelings and all of the senses consumed by love.

To take care of going overboard and to the extreme in the chase, hunt, search and quest of fun, amusement, thrills and delights because one can have such a good time that one does not desire to do anything else.

One Who Feels . . .

Sensual, love is in bloom, like holding hands or being close to another or holding another near and dear.

Aroused emotions, excited, tender, senses being stirred by another; inspired, affected, moved and impressed with powerful love feelings.

Like giving gifts or presents to another.

Treating someone to a meal or throwing a party for another.

One May Attract . . .

A social life with many balls, shindigs, coming out parties or debuts.

A date, engagement or appointment that can be pleasant or profitable.

Pleasure, joy.

A sweetheart, lover, suitor, beloved, a true love or infatuation, a beautiful love with warm and sensuous feelings. (Venus represents love and sensuality rather than physical sex . . . however, the sensual feelings and responses are a part of the physical sex act; physical sex is ruled by Mars.)

Type of People . . .

One who uses the actions and traits listed under the harmonious side of Venus, or whose hobby and/or work deals with anything listed under the harmonious side of Venus.

Loved one, companion, deb, debutante, socialite, jet set, high society, café society, the smart set, the social register, blue bloods, the elite, the one in love, patron of the arts.

One Whose Hobby and/or Work Deals With . . .

Anything listed under the harmonious side of Venus.

Fine arts, painting, drawing, sketching, illustration, sculpturing, ceramics, objects of art, water colorist, pottery, curios, statues, carvings, devising architectural plans, crafts, decorating, designing, engravings.

Fashion business, clothes, jewelry, purses, shoes, millinery, hats, accessories, gloves, personal adornment, trinkets, jewels, precious stones, rhinestones, beads, sequins, feathers, furs, wigs.

Hair colorist, salon operator, manicure, pedicure, nail polish, beauty treatment, cosmetics, perfume.

Ornaments, trimming things, window dressing.

Pastry, candy, sweets, desserts.

Flowers.

Gifts.

Dolls, puppets.

Poetry.

Music (listening to), concerts, singing (also Mercury), dancing.

Amusement, entertainment, fun and games, merriment, hobbies, holidays, sports (the fun part).

Modeling.

Going to movies, fashion shows, art galleries.

Parties, social gatherings, mixing and visiting with people, relaxation, resorts, being a host or hostess or doing it as a profession, cocktail parties, greeting and welcoming people, receptions (office, formal, official), interviewing (also the Moon), making appointments (for self or others), sending invitations (parties, weddings, showers).

Discordant Venus

One Who . . .

Grasps, seizes, selects and takes the direction or pursuit of the lowest amount of opposition.

May make love without loving the other person but he wants the other person to love him because he craves to be loved.

Draws, entices, tempts, beckons and uses a come-on to make people love him.

Gravitates toward doing wrong things which involve the affections; takes a certain path or course which may lead to immorality, debauchery and too much self-gratification.

Doesn't want to hurt another's feelings so gives in to another . . . one may not want to attend a party, dinner or social event but to avoid hurting someone's feelings will go against own desires . . . one that does this is usually angry with self because one is so weak and can't say no to others.

One Who Is . . .

Too permissive.

Too pliable, supple, flexible, pliant, submissive, yielding, soft, bending, easy (with people or relationships); readily influenced.

Overly zealous to satisfy or enchant others.

Overly affable, amiable, chummy, intimate, friendly, congenial, familiar, companionable, sociable, or overly wishful, wantful, eager and ambitious to satisfy, suit, charm, delight and fulfill others (the reason for this is because one wants to be loved by everyone. Therefore, one goes out of the way to obtain love for one's own satisfaction and it will be toward anyone who appears to be interested in the individual).

Loose, immoral, licentious, undiscriminating, promiscuous, immodest or playing at love.

A flirt, coquette, Lothario, Don Juan, Casanova (also Neptune; Venus is the desire for affection).

Dissipated, depraved, jaded, blase, lewd, libertine, lascivious, wanton, a trollop (one desires love so much that one will stoop to any level to have it).

Showy, flashy, gaudy, garish, unrefined, unpolished.

Pliable and submissive toward love and willingly, promptly or quickly gives in to ease or the easy way out with the object of her affections.

Indulged, humored, spoiled, coddled.

Generous with love or the loved one.

Big-hearted in being alive, existing and with romantic matters.

Too sensitive, excessively and extremely touchy, thin-skinned, susceptible and responsive.

Unfortunate with ardor, infatuation, desire, affection or romance.

Easily moved or aroused by strong feelings.

Ill-advised.

Senseless, silly (when in love).

Careless of habits, sloppy, slothful.

Lazy, shiftless, inactive, passive, languid, lackadaisical.

Too quiet.

Unhurried, a slow-poke; a dawdler, a dillydallier, a loiterer, constantly lounging around doing nothing.

Unthinking, neglectful, slack and thoughtless with outlay, disbursements, expenses, costs, prices, luxuries or overhead.

One Who Desires . . .

To please others rather than have a fight (quarrel) because one loves peace, harmony and beauty in one's surroundings and would do almost anything to attain these desires.

Approval from others.

Fun, pleasure, amusements or luxuries.

To overdo and overly enjoy entertainment and having a good time; to do too much socializing and at a fast pace.

One Who Has ...

Upset, uneasy, perturbed, bothered or disturbed feelings due to love matters.

Social boredom.

A touchy reaction to mythical, fabricated, made up or real snubs, scorns, disdains, slights and/or resistance that makes one place one thing in contrast or against another; feelings easily hurt.

Difficulty with putting into words, voicing, revealing, showing and exhibiting feelings, emotions, sentiments, fondness, tenderness and love nature.

A loved one hurt feelings.

Misunderstandings and disagreements with the object of one's affections.

Unlimited sensibility and feeling.

An inclination or impulse to be self-gratifying, free-living or dissipating.

Intemperance in fun, amusements, entertainments, thrills and sensualness.

Little strength or control regarding right and wrong in human conduct (mainly with fun and pleasure or involving the affections).

Bad taste that is the opposite of accepted standards, poor quality, inferior or unprincipled or poor judgement in selecting, matching or harmonizing things (this is seen in a gaudy dresser or painting . . . art work . . . with poor color combinations or poor harmony and form).

Inelegance in culture, the artistic and in selecting, matching or harmonizing things (objects, items).

A yearning, devotion, fancy, attachment and super abundance of affection for affluence, richness, wealth, opulence.

A skin problem (blemishes, pimples . . . usually from too many sweets), or a hair problem.

One May Attract . . .

Problems with social functions, friendly parties, affairs or gatherings.

Problems with loved ones, companions.

Flattery.

Unpleasant, disagreeable, distasteful, objectionable, unacceptable, or uncomfortable adventures, escapades or ordeals with love affairs, romance or flirtations. The result may make one moved, stirred and concerned about everything that happens with affairs of the heart.

Type of People . . .

One who uses the actions and traits listed under the harmonious side of Venus negatively and/or who uses the actions and traits listed under the discordant side of Venus.

One whose hobby and/or work deals with anything listed under the harmonious or discordant side of Venus.

One Whose Hobby and/or Work Deals With . . .

Anything listed under the harmonious or discordant side of Venus.

Harmonious Mars

One Who . . .

Likes action.

Freely confronts hazards, perils, risks, pitfalls, chances, threats, ventures.

Triumphs over, gains, secures or prevails against a mission, object, end, purpose or aim.

Achieves, fulfills and attains aims, ambitions, purposes, targets.

Punches, nudges, shoves, prods, goads, inspires and pushes onward.

Proceeds, goes on, gains ground, forges ahead, presses onward, speeds, makes headway, dashes ahead, lunges forward and keeps going at full steam ahead.

Makes up for lost time, rushes around, buzzes about, darts to and fro.

Appears as if forever, perpetually and endlessly spinning, revolving or twirling.

Makes the most of one's time, makes hay while the sun shines, keeps the ball rolling.

Makes the sparks fly, hurries, scurries, says "Rush!, Make haste!, Hurry Up!, Right now!, On the double!, Step on it!, Get a move on!, Make it snappy!, Shake a leg!".

Wrangles, squabbles; scuffles.

Advances and charges against others.

Lays siege to, raids, invades; pulls a gun on, fires upon, stabs, sticks, pierces, knifes, gores, hurls at or throws at others (these activities may be attracted under the harmonious side of Mars . . . during war a soldier may become involved in these areas when defending the country; or a detective or bullfighter, because of profession, may use these energies).

Doesn't have a moment to spare or call his own; works too hard or works beyond need or appeal or who does tiring or additional labor (but he thrives under it).

Labors, operates, trades or moves in a rapid, quick and speedy manner.

Will not admit, receive or reconcile self to abide, tolerate, welcome or adopt setbacks, losing outcomes, vanquishments and hurdles.

Depends, trusts, relies on or has confidence in self; creates (brings into being, gives birth to, gives life to, composes, conceives).

Gives form to, molds, patterns, shapes, fashions and fabricates in his own creative manner.

Commences, launches, propels, begins, sets going an object, article, project or vision.

Constructs, builds, erects, engineers, remodels, rises above and wins over any hostility, competitor, aversion or antagonism.

One Who Is . . .

Fast in action and quick in performance, pursuits, movements, operations, achievements, undertakings and feats.

Drawn toward or around danger (and may thrive on it), brave, bold, unafraid, audacious, assured, dauntless, spunky, spirited, martial, valorous, intrepid, lion-hearted, chivalrous, assertive, positive, dogmatic, generous, impetuous, brusque, direct, straightforward.

Less, minus and/or absent of self-restraint, composure, constraint, shyness.

Without dread, doubt, apprehension, dismay, modesty or mousiness.

A live wire, full of life, an eager beaver, peppy, on the go and run, never idle, indefatigable.

Unyielding, unconceding, determined, set, stubborn, unpliable, inflexible.

Bustling about, in a whirl, dynamic, dashing, animated, productive, enterprising, adventuresome, fierce and intense in feeling or manner; zealous, fiery, vehement, passionate, fervent, red-hot.

One Who Desires . . .

To inaugurate, initiate, present, inject, interpose, and turnout products or become involved in projects which require producing or developing.

To dote on and enjoys a dare, query, challenge and will dispute and defy others so one can win and conquer.

To compete, to contest, to battle, grapple, wrestle (having fun doing so because one likes the struggle involved).

To break one's neck in trying to complete tasks.

Activity, movement, busyness, to scramble.

One Who Can . . .

Compete and who desires to win.

Lead in a pioneering fashion.

Make a stir, expedite things.

Prevail against, resist, oppose and defy weariness, tiredness, strain, stress, tension and overwork.

Withstand hardships, burdens, predicaments, problems, pitfalls, inconveniences.

Defy depression, dismay, disheartenment, dejection or hopelessness.

Withstand when others are in pain, cowering, cringing or wincing. (Physicians need this trait . . . they can operate under the harmonious side of Mars with skill, or a patient may have better success with an operation when it is performed under a harmonious Mars aspect, or a fighter has a better chance of winning . . . the preceding can still be successful under the discordant side of Mars but it is more difficult and a struggle may be involved.)

One Who Has . . .

Ability to overthrow, smash, overcome, defeat, conquer or triumph over foes and adversaries.

Blood and guts, valor, get up and go.

Tireless, unfailing, hardy and unwearied energy.

Grit, brass, nerve, zip, zing, punch, spunk, plenty to do, many irons in the fire, gumption, daring, boldness and bravery to risk money or take a risk in business.

A firm and intense impelling pressure and motivation toward work, a performance, pursuit or any deed that he desires to accomplish.

The ability to grasp or start new undertakings.

The desire, incentive or urge to create.

The sentiments, sensibilities and feelings moved, excited or inflamed; gratifying and fulfilling sex.

An accident.

Surgery.

One Who Feels . . .

Brisk, energetic, lively, vivacious, vibrant or aggressive.

Like diving and plunging into things without taking the time to think about them.

He must master, overcome, subjugate, win and be victorious.

He must voice, state, utter or say outwardly (without reserve) what he wants to say.

Like gambling and taking chances.

Like carrying out, engaging in and discharging things with little casualty, misfortune or repercussion.

A heat wave, hot and/or warm because of moving so fast.

Frantically exhilarated, stirred, aroused, awakened and stimulated, resulting in a great state of sexual frenzy. A torrid, erotic, or sexy feeling that may give one a thrilling, throbbing and tingling sensation which makes one feel in the mood for sex . . . with these feelings one can be satisfied sexually.

One May Attract . . .

Hazards, perils, pitfalls, risks and conflicts, dissensions, disagreements, frictions or fights, bouts, matches, tournaments, duels, fist-fighting or a knock-down, drag-out fight.

A rival, competitor.

A favorable time for surgery or anything that is cut, lanced or removed with a sharp instrument.

Safety in a hazardous venture.

An automobile accident (the damage may be more to the car; one may be fortunate and escape injury, or the injury may be minor).

Type of People . . .

One who uses the actions and traits listed under the harmonious side of Mars, or whose hobby and/or work deals with anything listed under the harmonious side of Mars.

Dare-devils, acrobats, high-wire or trapeze artists, lion or tiger trainers in the circus, athletes, sports participants, bodyguards, dancers, flame throwers, bull-fighters, those in the armed services, conquerors, police officers, fire fighters, truck drivers, movers, stevedores, engineers, mechanics, dentists, doctors, surgeons, heroes or heroines (the danger and adventure part).

One Whose Hobby and/or Work Deals With . . .

Anything listed under the harmonious side of Mars.

Creative enterprises.

Manufacturing, producing, industry.

Construction work that involves architecture, building, shaping, structure.

Destruction work that involves wreckage, demolition.

Arms, munitions, deadly weapons, armaments, swords, cannons, cartridges, torpedoes, arrows, darts, slingshots, all types of guns (pistols, revolvers, rifles), knives, spears, scissors, steel, machinery, tools, spark plugs, thumb tacks, nails, bombs, fires, fireworks, explosives.

Sporting or surgical equipment, instruments (sharp), needles, utensils.

Liquor.

Hot music (jazz or fast rhythm), marches, dancing (the muscular activity involved because Mars rules the muscles).

Endeavors, business, trade, pursuit, occupation, craft or toil which requires bodily strength to perform.

Baseball, football, golf, swimming, weight lifting, wrestling, drag racing, tennis, polo, hockey, basketball, running, jogging, exercising.

Sculpting (the creative energy employed as well as the muscles needed).

The military, war craft, police work.

Mathematics.

Competition.

Discordant Mars

One Who . . .

Does not use common sense or the usual logic, which results in fast reactions of rage, and therefore, pitfalls, predicaments, troubles, complications, inconveniences, wastes, defeats and failures may occur.

Behaves, conducts or reacts to unexpected, impulsive, quick, frenzied, absurd and insane urges, inclinations, motives and desires.

Quickly, without effort, becomes moved or excited by rage, fury, wrath, displeasure, hatred or hostility.

Wagers or takes a chance with risk of loss or uncertain gain.

Fails to keep a good nature, temperament, disposition, humor.

Easily becomes ablaze, burning and fiery.

Responds, recoils or flies back with a bad temper, anger, wrath or violence.

Does not think or figure anything out or does not analyze, con-clude or deduce things mentally . . . instead he reacts with temper and does things without thinking.

Fights, attacks, assaults, battles, wrecks, smashes, ruins, muti-lates, shatters, breaks, destroys or exterminates things.

Crushes, lacerates, rips or shreds articles or objects.

Brings about, brings on, makes, produces, creates, effectuates, prompts, inspires and evokes insults, outrages, breaches of law, infractions, violations, transgressions or wrongs.

Sets upon, assails, pounces on, charges, strikes or hits with his fist (an object or person).

Uses blasphemous or sacrilegious language.

Dissipates, wastes, squanders and fritters away his endurance, energy, pep, fortitude or money (the money if the second house is involved in the aspect).

Toys or plays with any inflamed or combustible objects, plays with fire and gets his fingers burned (this may be with a physical attraction, or a child who plays with matches).

Fumes, raves, rants, kicks up a row, stamps one's feet in anger, flames up, snaps at others, becomes mad or sore, jumps down another's throat, takes one's anger out on others, allows one's passions to rise.

One Who Is . . .

Eager to harm, wound, affront, outrage or offend others.

Incensed, constantly arguing, bickering or wrangling with others.

In discordance and disharmony with another.

Furious with self or others.

Involved in deeds, exploits, actions or performances of fury, rage or passion which could involve infringement or illegal activity.

Constantly moving about and may annoy others by pacing the floor, or playing musical chairs (also Mercury-hopping from one chair to another; Mars is the physical energy part).

Burns, scalds, singes or cuts oneself or others.

Hot-tempered, hot-blooded, peppery, spunky.

Unpleasant, unlikable.

Flushed with anger, in a huff, in a rage, storming, mad as a hornet, boiling mad, fit to be tied, crude, unrefined, ill-bred, uncivil, rude, rough, unpolished, coarse, impolite, unmannerly, ill-behaved, discourteous, disrespectful, uncultured, saucy, sassy, unruly, ill-tempered, scornful, derisive, brash, disdainful, ungentle, abusive, ill-treating of others, piercing.

A hellion, hellcat, vixen, shrew, a holy terror, tough, a brow-beater, aiming blows at others, irate.

Like a tempest, tornado, gust, cyclone.

Hard, spiteful, not obliging, outrageous, flippant, jealous, callous, incautious, ferocious, a barbarian, insulting, vicious, malicious, spiteful.

Wicked, evil, nasty, horrid, vile, savage, brutal, primitive, sadistic (also Pluto), inhuman, unmerciful, merciless, pitiless, remorseless, insensitive to pain in others or to the feelings of others.

Obnoxious, repulsive, vulgar, immodest, unashamed, unembarrassed, bold, daring, assuming, forward, unabashed, immoral, unchaste.

Nervy, bare-faced, tactless, inconsiderate, thoughtless, neglectful, imprudent, careless, reckless, heedless, hare-brained, unthinking, misguided, slack.

Boisterous, rowdy, brazen, noisy, disorderly, relentless, antagonistic.

Disloyal, untrustworthy, treacherous, not submissive, belligerent, self-willed, obstinate, stubborn, uncontrollable, contrary, disagreeable, annoying, provoking, argumentative, contentious, quarrelsome, testy.

A fighter, a brawler, a scrapper, vindictive, anxious to get even.

Unrelaxed, in constant motion, overly hurried, rushed or speedy in action with an inability or unwillingness to endure delay or interruptions, in too much of a hurry to get everything done right now (which can create problems, setbacks, struggles or accidents), hasty or rash in action, impulsive.

Overly aggressive, strong, powerful (from energy), dynamic, rampant, fast, tempestuous.

Over-sexed, lustful, animalistic, passionate, inflamed, fiery, fervent, warm, amorous with sexual desire and satisfaction, sensual in a sexual way, lecherous, overly arduous.

Saturated and charged with abhorrence, detestation, loathing or abomination.

Temperamental.

Energetic in any pursuit or vocation.

Intoxicated, impaired.

One Who Desires . . .

To use physical force on another.

Thrills and excitement, perhaps from pornographic books, objects or photography (Mercury = books; Neptune = photography—obscenity is Mars as well as the sexual part).

Yearns for a lark, experience or escapade.

One Who Can . . .

Cuss, curse, swear.

Originate or create an uproar, pandemonium, tumult, commotion, racket, rumpus or turbulence with loudness, rudeness or temper.

Fly off the handle, blow a fuse, blow one's top (stack), erupt like a volcano, go on a rampage.

Spend or use an enormous amount of physical energy.

Over-work beyond need or necessity.

Become debauched.

Be extremely passionate.

One Who Has . . .

A blaze of temper and becomes infuriated, enraged or in an uproar.

An unnatural rage.

Clashes or rifts with others.

A despise or contempt for others.

No reflection, consideration or reasoning for the end result of any action taken.

Demonstrative, stirring and temperamental outbursts, outbreaks, eruptions, explosions.

Temper tantrums, fits.

Ungovernable, swift and unruly flare-ups, blowups; backfires.

Stormy scenes.

An argument, fracas, riot, feud, vendetta, dispute, conflict, dissension, strife, a quibble, a debate.

Active opposition, resistance and a violent impact of two moving bodies (people or vehicles).

Hazardous, dangerous and/or speculative enterprises, endeavors, undertakings and business.

Real and/or factual perils, jeopardies, pitfalls, mishaps, accidents, fires.

Fever, temperature, heatstroke, rupture.

An infection; an inflamed condition of the muscles or joints accompanied by pain, redness, heat and swelling; any disease or infection that is infectious, communicable, transferrable.

Surgery, a lancing.

One May Attract ...

An immense battle with people or one's desires.

Anything that brings bodily harm (fights, stabbings, pistol shots, accidents) or one may be the instigator of these things.

Problems and difficulties which may result in loads of trouble, and wrongdoings that one may not be able to get away with because they most likely will be discovered.

Mechanical devices which may fail, collapse, fracture in pieces or are not useable or in working condition.

Type of People ...

One who uses the actions and traits listed under the harmonious side of Mars negatively and/or who uses the actions and traits listed under the discordant side of Mars.

One whose hobby and/or work deals with anything listed under the harmonious or discordant side of Mars.

An arsonist.

One Whose Hobby and/or Work Deals With ...

Anything listed under the harmonious or discordant side of Mars.

Harmonious Jupiter

One Who ...

Relies on aid, support, benevolence or kindly feelings of others.

Seems and looks unconcerned, unbothered and undistressed.

Divides in fair and equal parts, distributes, gives to others.

Profits by, is helpful to, partakes in and divides equally with others.

Delights in, relishes and is fond of accommodating and supporting people.

Bestows, awards and gives another accommodation.

Benefits others.

Spreads and emits kindness, sympathy, pity and good wishes for others.

Loans, advances, aids or accommodates as a favor to another.

Spreads cheer, gives hope, inspires, reassures, raises, elevates and glorifies others.

Directs, leads, guides and handles concerns, interest, business, work, projects and undertakings in a big way.

Yields to or bestows upon others a beneficial exchange.

Sees things through rose-colored glasses.

Takes a cheerful and hopeful view of life with an attitude of "all is for the best."

Gives, shares and bestows bliss, cheer, gaiety, joy and well-being to others.

Goes along with people or situations.

Uses discretion.

Donates or grants things to others.

Acts in a proper or suitable manner and is favored in his intentions and expressions.

Spreads sunshine, indulges in fun, plays pranks, makes jokes, beams, grins, laughs.

Wishes and wants to cause others to be contented, delighted, elated and glad.

Will voluntarily and gladly take a monetary gamble, a chance or speculate. Does not feel like doing humdrum, ordinary work or a servant's job because of feeling above that; must have a profession.

Looks forward to everything that life has to offer.

Believes in religion.

One Who Is . . .

A giver.

Magnanimous.

Charitable.

Open-handed.

Big-hearted, good-hearted, good-natured, ungrudging.

Bountiful, generous.

Broad-minded, liberal, tolerant, impartial, uncalculating, lenient, easygoing, aspiring, permissive, complacent, obliging, hearty, sincere, open-minded, understanding, impartial, honest, ethical, upstanding, above-board, on the up-and-up, truthful.

Just, fair, equitable, decent.

Willing to help and be a friend.

Hospitable, cordial, affable, cheerful, chummy, gregarious, unaffected, hopeful, contented, zealous, happy, smiling, radiant, genial, jovial, festive, lively, bubbling, twinkling, jocular, hilarious, glowing, candid, merry, fun, fervent, sportsmanlike, pleasurable, a prankster, a funster, giggly, a good neighbor (in attitude), an optimist.

Flamboyant, an extrovert.

Funny, comical, jolly, gleeful, priceless.

Excellent or admirable at vending, marketing, merchandising or selling.

Rich, affluent, prosperous, well-fixed, well-to-do, opulent, well-heeled, wealthy or has substantial money.

Assured, poised.

Expectant, constant, true, unfailing; reliant.

Complies with and abides by rules, ordinances, regulations, decrees, commandments and by-laws (due to the desire to do right, be honest or to be fair).

Honest and impartial in performance, execution, action, decisions, undertakings and amusements.

Agreeable, pleasant, reliable.

Readily, freely and cheerfully desirous of submitting to and tolerating regulations, laws, customs, codes, protocol and disciplines (even if the price is enormous).

Dedicated and partially or entirely gives up one's time, business or material desires in order to devote one's life to a person, task or religion.

Engaged in a learned vocation, speciality or career and ministers, helps, aids, answers and/or provides something to others.

Pious, devout, God-fearing, saintly, orthodox.

Interested in philosophy.

Elaborate, an exhibitionist (in a manner that does not cause dislike).

One Who Desires . . .

To live it up and have a ball.

To have an outlay of money so one can devote and pass time on self-gratification, free living, dissipation, luxuries, expensive and costly expenditures, entertainment or amusements.

To exhibit and show conspicuously self or material assets.

To be the center of attention (from a friendly, amusing and fun standpoint).

To be unselfish.

To be lavish.

Wealth.

One Who Can . . .

Do things with a flourish.

Be attracted to pageantry or things that are showy, swank, grand, and may splurge on them or self.

Gain or have an upturn of good things such as money or business, which may pick up, grow, mount and be boosted upwards.

Hike up prices.

Attract extra money.

Build a home addition, enlarge an office or expand a business.

One Who Has . . .

Kind feelings.

A "share the wealth" philosophy.

His economy multiply.

The desire, stimulus, impulse and propulsion to increase, distend and widen things.

His hopefulness, buoyancy and merriment enhanced, heightened or boosted.

Good thinking, rational, analytical, inductive and deductive reasoning.

Excellent, admirable and worthy conclusions, decisions and opinions.

An outgoing and friendly disposition, outlook, air, bearing.

A natural impulse of extending self to others.

The ability to encourage others by giving reassurance.

An ease and peace that makes others desirous of being in one's presence.

Appreciates and comprehends anything that appeals to the sense of the comic and provokes mirth.

Conduct, bearing, carriage, manner, morals and behavior affected, moved, impressed, swayed, governed and inspired when thinking, reflecting, contemplating and speculating with feelings of deep respect, reverence or devotion for a person or thing.

A towering feeling, impression and sensitivity of obligation, responsibilities, services, trusts, tasks, business.

An unruffled, tranquil, quiet, composed, enduring, lasting and continuous trust, confidence, allegiance, belief, piety, creed; hopeful theories on life.

A dependence upon a religious faith, a Supreme Deity, Holy Spirit, God, or Almighty Creator.

Divine protection.

One May Attract . . .

Success and/or a thriving business.

A raise, step up, addition or increase involving investments, money or a business.

Favorable investment areas.

Aid and support from those who have prestige, authority, power or wealth.

Those with affluence or plenty.

Access, additions, expansions, enlargements, increase and/or growth developments or unfoldments.

Compromises with others.

People who feel like engaging, hiring or using one's help, assistance and/or employment (others like one's friendly manner).

Others who are fond of, enjoy and partial to one and react with kindness, accommodation or benefits.

Fortunate events.

Prosperity, riches, fortune or a treasure—dependent upon other aspects, one's environment and what one is doing to gain riches, because one will not be rich if one is not in the proper environment and area to make money, unless one inherits (eighth house) or receives it through a marriage or business partner (eighth house).

Favorable legal matters (if the seventh and ninth houses do not have conflicting discordant aspects).

Type of People ...

One who uses the actions and traits listed under the harmonious side of Jupiter, or whose hobby and/or work deals with anything listed under the harmonious side of Jupiter.

Ministers, priests and rabbis.

Astrologers.

Psychologists, marriage counselors, consultants.

Lawyers.

Bankers, financiers.

Publishers.

The jet set.

One Whose Hobby and/or Work Deals With ...

Anything listed under the harmonious side of Jupiter.

Metaphysics.

Philosophical areas.

Religion.

Banking, finances.

Merchandising, selling

Investments.

Shipping.

Importing, exporting.

Publishing.

Commerce, capitalism, raising of revenue.

Expensive items.

The courts.

Displays, exhibits.

The business field.

The professions.

Counseling (anyone who gives advice, listens to or encourages others).

A bedside manner (doctors may have this).

Making people like and respond to one (politicians do this . . . the kissing of babies and shaking of hands technique).

The ornate, baroque, deluxe, rich, plush.

Jade, tin.

Discordant Jupiter

One Who . . .

Goes on boisterous, frolics, larks, antics, adventures, escapades.

Desires to socialize, party, entertain and fritter away, squander or waste his time, money, pep and stamina.

Tries to impress people with splendor, lavishness or wealth.

Devises, organizes or arranges expensive undertakings, amusements or entertainment.

Spends money on overly expensive items that later may prove

not to be worth the price paid.

Refuses to and hesitates to view, estimate, appraise or take into account prices, charges, rates and expenditures.

Gratifies one's tastes and desires in a showy, flashy, flamboyant, glitter and pretentious way by wasteful show, spread, exhibit or spectacle.

Feels pleasure or happiness, and is enraptured and content when spending money on others or if sharing it with another.

Thinks he is Santa Claus and goes beyond his means in gratifying his tastes and desires.

Repulses and rebuffs people with money, affluence, riches, assets or resources.

Desires to exhibit, parade and blaze in view of others.

Feels like a king who revels in luxury, pomp and plush surroundings and who has little or no feeling for those lower in rank or position (if one takes this attitude, one is most likely to attract difficulties with others).

Blows one's own horn or trumpet.

Flatters oneself, pats oneself on the back, self-applauds, self-praises (for extroversion and overconfidence reasons).

Overly assumes, accepts or appropriates things to, or upon oneself.

Magnifies, overestimates, overstates, stretches a point, exaggerates, talks big; goes beyond, extends or reaches too far in one's aims, desires, plans or deals.

Manifests, signifies, suggests and uses poor taste or lacks discrimination with decisions, opinions, appraisals or assessments.

Performs or renders tricks, jokes or mischief on others.

Overdoes everything, including eating, playing, sex.

Doesn't measure food when cooking . . . the ingredients are poured or thrown in and/or are in large pieces.

Deviates from recipes and adds extra amounts or extra ingredients.

Over-feeds others, likes to have enough food to feed an army.

Likes, relishes and is fond of fatty, oily, lardy, buttery or overly spiced or seasoned foods.

Likes condiments, rich foods or fluffy, creamy, rich sauces.

Gorges, packs, jams food down in a hoggish or piggish manner.

Doesn't save left-overs and is wasteful with food.

One Who Is . . .

Desirous of making money for self and others, regardless if the other people involved are financially ruined.

Far out and overly desirous for advancement, wealth, honor or power; overly trustful and anticipates too much in return.

Too reliant upon the words of others.

Lacking selectivity.

Not alert, astute, bright, clever, perceptive, shrewd or wide awake and does not use rational reasoning or a careful examination of the direction in which one is headed.

Overly confident in hopes and has a rosy outlook.

Overly certain, positive and definite.

Too hopeful and cheerful in believing things are alright in life.

Overly dependent on, leans on, counts on, banks on and believes in excellent, admirable, worthy and first-rate concepts, views, judgments, estimations, conclusions of others or fortune, luck, possibility, opportunity, odds or risks.

Naive, too trusting.

Impulsive.

Led and steered by emotions, sentiments, sympathies, pathos or affection and impressions; overly eager.

Too enthusiastic and carefree.

Overly zealous.

Crazy or wild about plans or people.

Fun-loving, frolicsome, merry, playful.

Foolish, overly liberal, too generous.

Dissipated, impractical, self-gratifying, free-living.

Excessively, exceedingly and extremely big-hearted, unselfish or charitable; a feigner of great, magnificent and majestic traits, characteristics, goodness or worth.

Self-important, conceited, showy, boastful, blusterous, overly assured, expectant.

Always taking others for granted.

Unthinking, unmindful of or thoughtless of others.

One Who Has . . .

No concern, regard, worry, anxiety or responsibility in outlook, disposition or habitude.

Expensive, costly and high expenditures.

The impression that one is obligated or required to be generous, lavish, open-handed, extravagant, bountiful, unthrifty or uncurbed with spending.

An exaggerated self-esteem and vanity because one likes to overdo things or be extroverted, or is over-confident.

Individual and exclusive affairs, pursuits and undertakings done in excess.

An "I don't care" attitude.

Viewpoints on life, ideology, creed, faith or religion that create problems with others.

Overconfidence with selling and expects more in return than what is actually received.

Ungrounded, illogical and mistaken hopefulness and a buoyant view of life.

Irrational, not sensible, senseless, unreasonable, unhealthy and insane enterprises, endeavors, undertakings or business deals.

Excessive and unneeded or inessential expenses, outlays, costs, outgo, splurges, squanderings or wastes.

Quick, hurried and speedy conclusions, decisions, opinions, verdicts, findings.

Business increases, growth, development that are uncertified, unassured and not guaranteed.

A disposition, outlook and habitude which could attract one to things that are illegal and cause one to be heedless of law.

One May Attract ...

Other people who charge him excessively or unreasonable amounts or more than is just.

Vows, engagements, commitments or contracts which may be made by oneself or others and these may not be maintained, performed, rendered or done.

Unfavorable conditions if one enlarges, increases or opens any new undertaking, pursuit, venture, affair, trade, dealing or transaction (one is overconfident and may do things in an enormous or huge way; the overhead may be higher than the profit).

People who may take advantage of one's pleasant demeanor, willingness to spend and congenial temperament . . . these people may endeavor to seize a favor, benefit or profit from him; an overabundance, oversupply, overflow and redundance of everything in undertakings, pursuits, dealings, interests, transactions or ventures.

Added body weight due to over-eating, or rich or fatty foods, parties and folly.

Type of People ...

One who uses the actions and traits listed under the harmonious side of Jupiter negatively and/or who uses the actions and traits listed under the discordant side of Jupiter.

One whose hobby and/or work deals with anything listed under the harmonious or discordant side of Jupiter.

One Whose Hobby and/or Work Deals With ...

Anything listed under the harmonious or discordant side of Jupiter.

Harmonious Saturn

One Who . . .

Feels like saving things.

Must have things stored or laid away for necessity or future use.

Desires to have something (money, education or a person) to fall back upon.

Dislikes waste.

Puts value on matters (material possessions or objects) rather than the spiritual.

Feels inferior.

May take his time doing something.

Has a dearth of ideas.

Pays attention to regular duties or work.

Exchanges or patronizes others.

Vends, markets or merchandises by offering a sale, a low or budget price.

Buys something at an inexpensive price.

Cuts back or rolls back the price.

Bows to others.

Appears like he has a hard shell or is a hard nut to crack.

Keeps things within and does not show emotions, sentiments or sympathies; does not respond to impressions or thoughts.

Looks before leaping.

Takes precautions.

Limits, restricts, controls, denies and disciplines self.

Supports or provides for others (as a duty).

Hides.

Punches a clock.

Sticks to schedules and enjoys doing so.

Preserves material objects.

Economizes.

Has a stockpile accumulated or desires to accumulate a stockpile (may be money, material objects, food, etc.).

Mends, fixes, repairs, restores, overhauls, corrects, remakes, re-
builds, recasts, remodels, reconstructs, renews, renovates, re-
habilitates, redecorates.

Re-does things over and over again.

Rehearses (like an opera singer that rehearses for hours).

Saves everything because he never knows when an item will be
useful.

Sticks to standards and standard methods of doing things (for example, when cooking, one uses the *exact* ingredients and
measures or weighs everything . . . does not deviate from the
recipe, follows it completely . . . afraid to deviate because
maybe it will not turn out right; he doesn't add extra amounts
of food because he can't stand waste or doesn't like leftovers,
but will save leftovers . . . this type cook may have enough
food for everyone to have one serving . . . this would also be
dependent upon other aspects in the chart and may be more
predominate with a discordant Saturn).

One Who Is . . .

Practical and may have sound, although conservative, business
policies,

Sensible, sane, matter of fact, rational, definite, specific,
down-to-earth, realistic, moderate.

Economical, frugal.

Able to put things into shipshape condition.

Thorough in tasks.

Efficient, well-ordered, proficient, able, firm, solid, dependable,
unchanging, unvarying, unwavering, constant, responsible,
stable, believable.

Trustworthy, true blue, unfailing, diligent.

Precise, sharp and promptly on time.

Inflexible, unbending.

Unyielding in toil, pursuit, profession, chore, skill, labor and endeavor.

Competent to conduct and convey a charge or duty and ready in accepting duty.

Cautious, careful, judicious.

Skilled in negotiation.

Adroit, adept, practiced, aimful, wise, profound, discerning, patient.

Well-balanced, cool-headed, restrained, well-behaved, docile, humble, unpretentious.

Quiet, shy, plain, simple, unassuming, introverted, recessive, mousy, placid.

Noiseless, soundless, hushed, at rest, at peace, composed, self-collected, unflustered.

Detached, inaccessible, remote, silent, bashful, inhibited, undemonstrative, unaffectionate, difficult to understand, a wallflower, unsociable, elusive, close-lipped, fearful people won't like him.

Wary, cagey, heedful, cautious, watchful, on guard, alert.

Mindful, attentive, penetrating, perceptive, able to get to the base or foundation of things, on the lookout, protective (from a safety standpoint), security conscious.

Aware of and appreciative of shelter, safety, collateral and protection.

Staunch, immovable, uncompromising, resolved in his ways, stubborn, persistent, retentive.

Unmerciful, unrelenting, pitiless, stiff, firm, strict, literal.

Rigorous, willful, purposeful, persevering, consistent, trite, monotonous, dull, boring, unoriginal.

Simple to the point of severity, staid, sober, demure, calm, serious, solemn, grim, somber,

Earnest, rightful, correct, proper, moral, square (called by hip people), puritanical, prudish, prissy, prim, modest, respectful.

Unromantic, unsentimental, unimaginative, stuffy, traditional, orthodox, pious, meditative, wistful, melancholic, inactive, retiring.

Evasive, furtive, secretive, discreet, uncommunicative.

Able to teach, instruct or school self.

Weak-kneed, inferior, lowly, shabby, backward, under par, sub-ordinate, uncluttered, neat (a person may appear shabby in at-tire and be neat with the labor performed).

One Who Can . . .

Initiate, introduce and launch techniques, theories, ways and means or short cuts that save money and cut down on cost.

Buy, swap, barter, trade, accumulate money or material posses-sions.

Retain things and amass, collect or store products, money or a nest egg.

Gather things for later use.

Forfeit, give up and relinquish things because of necessity or be-cause one knows it will be beneficial in the future.

Gain what is deserved or merited.

See things beforehand and use pre-consideration.

Bide his time with calm endurance and without complaining.

Lie in wait.

Stay in the background, take a back seat to others, play second fiddle.

Endure plenty.

Use common sense.

Use preconception, forethought, foreknowledge or premedita-tion.

Watch people, birds, etc.

Keep one's distance.

Make sure of others or conditions.

Keep things under lock and key.

Stick to the facts.

Record things in detail.

Concentrate attention in one area.

Put things in their proper prospective.

Explore, examine or conduct a searching inquiry into affairs or conditions.

Comply and submit to the principles, regulations, formulas, routines, customs, orders, codes or protocol that others make.

Reject extravagant and useless expenditures and projects.

Inflict isolation, quiet or seclusion on oneself because of a desire to do so.

One May Attract . . .

More tasks, chores, endeavors, undertakings or added charges, duties or obligations to be reliable and accountable for, or thrifty, careful administration of the affairs of the household, business or community.

A favorable time for laying out money in expectation of profit if the gain from it is a gradual, definite and positive process, or if the deal does not ripen or develop too rapidly.

An auspicious time to make eventful, grave, serious, major and weighty conclusions, determinations, settlements, rulings, findings, decrees, judgments, verdicts or resolutions.

Favorable conditions with actual and concrete holdings, belongings or assets.

A good time for bargains.

Pleasant dealings with the establishment.

Delays, postponements, restrictions, constrictions, interferences, snags, hitches, retardations, impediments or hindrances . . . they may be long or temporary delays, waitings, laggings or stallings . . . but there is a good reason for the problems and it is usually to one's advantage to patiently wait for the outcome.

Type of People . . .

One who uses the actions and traits listed under the harmonious side of Saturn, or whose hobby and/or work deals with anything listed under the harmonious side of Saturn.

Junk dealer.

Janitor.

Caretaker, custodian.

Warden.

Guardian.

Guard, watchman, patrol officer.

Chaperone.

The old, aged, senior citizen or a person older than oneself.

The bourgeois class.

Farmer.

Judge, lawyer.

Engineer.

Buyer.

Architect.

Chemist (also Pluto).

Dentist (also Mars), doctor (also Mars), plastic surgeon (also Mars; Saturn is the reconstruction part).

Musician (needs Saturn to practice).

One Whose Hobby and/or Work Deals With . . .
Anything listed under the harmonious side of Saturn.

Real estate, property, land, acreage, tracts.

Sand, dirt, gravel, dryness, barren.

The earth.

The ground (digging, sowing).

Agriculture, harvests, commodities, hay, grain, coal, timber, lumber, rye, barley, oats, millet, soybeans, wheat.

Quarry, rocks, ores, minerals, leads, mines, stones.

Basic supplies or provisions, stock in trade, assets, essential materials, tangibles.

Utilities.

Irrigation.

Preservatives in food to retard spoilage.

Putting up and storing jams, preserves, pickles, etc.

Inexpensive products, cheap items, sales, bargains, wholesale, second hand clothes (also Venus).

Museums.

Warehouses.

Blue chips (stock or stock of established and old companies).

Collecting stamps, shells, antiques, treasures, coins.

Keeping things safe, safety deposit box.

Custody, protectorship.

Care, charge, guidance.

Defending, shielding, screening, safe-conduct of others.

Undercover work (also Pluto and twelfth house).

Safety glass.

Management, administration (organizing part).

Allocating resources, making an itemized and proportional plan for spending.

Laying out plans, formulas, routines, usages.

Arranging, grouping and structuring of a business or company.

The extreme limit or extent of being precise, exact or accurate.

Detailed correctness, exclusion of error.

Flawless, impeccable, pure, unblemished, unmarred.

Balancing, offsetting, surveying, gauging and marking all toils, labors and exertions.

Reckoning, appraising, evaluating, sizing, figuring.

Facts.

Technicalities, specifications.

Charting and plotting crusades, expeditions, trips, campaigns or a series of business operations for a stated purpose.

Using reason and being within practical bounds.

Reasonable, fair and legitimate conclusions.

Preparing reports.

Dense, confined and studious, considered, mindful, concentrated reflection, care and scrutiny to particulars, facts, schedules, circumstances and fine points.

Toiling and laboring by using patience and doing things slowly.

Scrupulous, meticulous and punctilious in technique, formula, practice or habit.

Tedious, uninteresting, unrelieved, fatiguing, wearisome, humdrum and diligent work.

Preparing cases, reports.

Ancient things (archaeology).

Saving lives, teeth, health.

Business deals that are brought about by conferring with another.

Discordant Saturn

One Who . . .

Suppresses, represses, restrains and controls innermost feelings and thoughts.

Enlarges, aggrandizes and exaggerates importance to the point of where one feels the need for individual, distinct, unique but just and decent treatment from others.

Dwells too long on his problems.

Takes alarm at the least little thing that occurs.

Recoils, flinches and is unwilling to take on ponderous, weighty and burdensome accountabilities, liabilities, responsibilities, encumbrances, duties or obligations . . . in fact, refuses to take them on.

Frets, fusses.

Puts things off, takes time or waits for others who are slow.

Always thinks of how he is affected rather than how the other person is affected.

Others shun because no one wants to be around him as he is too negative and selfish.

Looks on the worst side of things.

Lacks confidence.

Can't get out of the settled way of thinking or doing things.

Constantly calculates against others for self-interest.

Figures and premeditates misdeeds toward another with selfish hopes that the results will be in his favor.

Employs strategy and makes use of and adopts trickery or deception.

Defends, serves to protect, calculates to resist attack.

Uses others with selfish intent and for his own gain, benefit or profit.

Stores and accumulates objects, furnishings or belongings . . . he doesn't use them as they are his security.

Dreads, fears and dislikes extravagance, dissipation, squandering or lavishness.

Senses he is helpless which means (to his way of thinking) he is incapable of chores, duties or tasks; grumbles.

Whimpers, yowls, cries, broods, complains, mutters, snivels, bellyaches, panics.

Avoids, evades, shuns and neglects data, statistics, actuality or anything existing.

Restrains, holds in, smothers or conceals his emotions, affections, impressions and responses for dread of being injured, harmed, offended, rejected or hurt; tolerates and sanctions others to mar, harm and prejudice his emotions, sentiments or sensitivity.

Compels himself to make sacrifices and do without things, scrimps, saves and goes without the proper food.

Doesn't eat much.

Doesn't talk much.

Lacks riches, resources, substance, capital, holdings or money.

Dislikes the establishment (the upper middle class that are conventional, materialistic, stable, dutiful and proper).

One Who Is . . .

Deficient and minus in self-assurance, his own ability or fitness.

Responsive, easily affected or offended by snubs, scorn, disdain, disregard, fault-finding, unfavorable comments or by being ignored or disapproved by others.

Shamefaced, embarrassed (also Sun . . . ego; Saturn . . . lack of confidence and feeling of inferiority).

Self-centered.

Small-minded, narrow-minded.

Fatalistic.

Hopeless.

Concerned, worried.

Hurt, humiliated.

Detained.

Afraid to take chances.

Penurious.

Bankrupt or fears he will be; destitute or fears that he will be.

Fearful of stirring, budging, deviating, varying or altering his actions or thoughts.

Looking at others for undisclosed, undivulged, hidden and secret reasons, purposes or incentives because he thinks that people are out to use him.

Lacking breadth of view.

Afraid to oppose conventions or habits.

Provincial.

Overly moderate.

A miser, cheap, penny-pinching, stingy, greedy for wealth.

Jealous, grudging.

Cunning, foxy, roughish, wily, sly, clever (from a premeditated and contriving manner).

Subtle.

Always planning and devising.

Sardonic, embittered.

Cool, chilly, frigid, lukewarm.

Casual.

Disinterested, indifferent, unconcerned, insensitive.

Piercing, biting.

Remorseful, penitent, repentant; contrite.

Unassured, without courage.

Disinclined, averse, unwilling and incapable of showing, revealing, displaying, voicing or venting his emotions externally or
superficially.

Fearful and apprehensive or proffering or contributing self.

Silent.

In need.

Self-destroying, hurtful, detrimental, harmful, abusive, damaging
to self, suicidal, masochistic.

Desolate, forlorn, mirthless, blissless, cheerless, disgruntled, dis-
affected, dismayed, in pain, misery, anguish, torment, distress, discomfort, torture, agony.

Deficient in warmth, sympathy, understanding and pity because
he is selfish and only interested in himself.

Within and inside the mind resigned and submissive to the fact
he is powerless, helpless and incapable of releasing, letting
go or abandoning that matter, person or animal that has been
lost, strayed, vanished, departed, forfeited, destroyed,
wrecked or ruined.

Oppressive.

Monotonous, dim-witted, uninteresting, stuffy (a stuffed shirt).

Overly heedful, wary, discreet or careful.

Impotent (powerless and the inability to have sex).

Overly unbelieving, incredulous or agnostic.

One Who Desires . . .

To enviously take from others (from a using people angle) or
that which belongs to another.

To escape or depart from fact, actuality, realness, truth or substance.

To do things he will later regret or feel guilty about.

Self-destruction, self-punishment.

One Who Can . . .

See only the murky, obscure, dismal, gloomy and dreary part of things or people; dwell on and mull over everything with sorrow or regret.

Be afraid of having losses.

Be dispossessed.

Be tired, nonchalant, bashful, too modest, reserved, unsocial, too mousy, too shy, too reticent, unaffectionate, seclusive.

Be deceitful, beguiling, scheming, dishonest, indirect, shifty, conscienceless, unprincipled.

Stall, procrastinate, bring delays or adjournments.

One Who Has . . .

A loss of weight.

A deficiency in his diet.

Aches and pains.

An overly tedious, uninteresting, dull, unrelieved or formulated schedule of work and home life.

A lack of training.

Difficulty in paying attention or giving heed to things which involve the mental processes.

Postponements or things may be momentarily at a standstill . . . this may place him in a depressed or worried state of mind.

Wear and tear on clothes or articles.

An unnecessary anxiety or solicitude.

Dread of the future.

A tendency for lateness, is behind in paying debts or payments to others that may be late, behind, delayed or lost.

To forfeit something and this creates woeful, sorry or sad feelings.

Hidden motives or purposes.

Steals.

Avoids notice so he can become involved in clandestine affairs.

Fines or penalties.

Occurrences that are his own undoing and downfall.

A tendency for self-dislike, self-hate, mental uneasiness.

One Who Feels . . .

Dull, drab.

Ill-at-ease, doubtful.

Frightened, scared, alarmed.

Unsure, dubious, indefinite, insecure.

Malcontented, displeased, disappointed.

Dejection, despair, desperation,

Frustrated, melancholy, disheartened, unhappy, sad, gloomy, lonely, low, dispirited, dissatisfied, sorry, dreary.

Exhausted, fatigued, weary, low energy (these feelings may come from negative thinking which can wear one out, or from improper eating habits).

He will never catch up with his work.

He is rejected when unattended, disregarded, uncared for, unheeded or if someone doesn't pay enough attention to him.

Confined, limited, restricted, hindered.

Incomplete with a loved one.

People do not measure up to his standards or that he doesn't come up to theirs.

That he is in want or that he is short on the basic necessities of living from day to day.

Weighty, ponderous and heavy hardships, loads, accountabilities, liabilities, responsibilities or encumbrances.

Sorry for himself because he has too much work and too many duties that he is obligated to take care of.

Everything is falling apart.

He's not making headway, advancing or stepping forward.

No improvement is in sight.

His enviable, preferable and advantageous aims and ambitions are too difficult, hard, complex, complicated and tough to obtain.

Life revolves around him rather than others.

His rightful and appropriate acknowledgment for his laudable, praiseworthy, creditable and deserving performance, pursuit, achievement, accomplishment or undertaking has not been properly recognized by others and that no one has given him a pat on the back.

His lot and portion in life is worse than others.

He has had an uncommon, rare, uncustomary and exceptionally difficult and trying time in his life . . . more so than others.

His firm, consistent and rigid learning and persevering exertion, toil and labor resulted in small and insignificant advantages, gains or profits.

A condition or position will arise that he is unable to manipulate, work, use or manage in a sufficient or superior manner.

He will fail because he is imperfect and deficient in knowledge, know-how and ability to perform such a task or to handle any situation which may arise.

Fearful and apprehensive of gambling and taking a chance of losing a safe, sure and secure income by quitting a job . . . therefore, he may not quit . . . instead he will stick to the job and complain about how much he abhors it.

He is subordinate, lesser, smaller, lower, poorer and below others in position, finance or personal everyday living; fright; dread; dismay; horror, poverty conscious.

One May Attract . . .

A fall.

Tedious events.

Things that turn out all wrong.

A depression, slump, deflation or shortage.

A salary cutback, a decrease in pay, a loss of income.

Deprivation or defeat, poverty.

Occurrences that are his own doing.

Failure or a fear that he will fail.

Snags or bottlenecks in his path.

Slight, insubstantial, meager and insignificant income or repayments which results in a negative feeling.

Difficulties with money that was placed into something where a profit was expected.

Casualties, injury or costs that can deprive him of things.

A bargain or a good sale but it may end up that the product was a lemon, a constant source of trouble or not worth the bargain price . . . repairs may be needed; difficulty with things which are repaired, fixed or mended and he has to take the item back.

Type of People . . .

One who uses the actions and traits listed under the harmonious side of Saturn negatively and/or who uses the actions and traits listed under the discordant side of Saturn.

One whose hobby and/or work deals with anything listed under the harmonious side of Saturn.

One Whose Hobby and/or Work Deals With . . .

Anything listed under the harmonious or discordant side of Saturn.

Harmonious Uranus

One Who . . .

Believes in civil liberty and civil rights.

Amends what is evil and wrong.

Corrects social wrongs and makes changes for the better.

Tries to make a person, object, belief or institution better by removing faults or flaws (this can be in any line of conduct or work . . . plastic surgery is one area).

Changes his sex through an operation and has no ill effects (also Mars . . . the operation; Uranus . . . the change, the new person, the unusual).

Stands apart, differs, varies and is distinguished from others.

Sets no pattern.

Reinvents self.

Advocates free and independent action of all individuals because he believes that everyone should exist as himself and do his own thing.

Does things differently from normal.

Does not believe his eyes, ears or senses with what people overwhelm him with.

Can become flabbergasted, bewildered, stunned, astounded, stupefied, amazed, thunderstruck and in awe.

Marvels, stares or gapes at another or the other person does it to him.

Takes others unawares or others take his breath away.

One Who Is . . .

Different from the mold, a freak (a thing or occurrence that is very unusual or irregular . . . an abnormally formed organism (also Neptune).

Gay (homosexual).

Quaint, outlandish, odd, strange, weird.

Phenomenal, unmatched, unequaled, unparalleled, peerless, uncommon, rare, exceptional, unusual, unique, not common but remarkable and extraordinary, first.

Inventive, ingenious, smart, bright, brainy, wide-awake, acute, intelligent, sharp, perceptive.

Contrary, variant, changing.

Abrupt, curt, brusque, intellectually fast and speedy.

Self-reliant, not controlled by another, free, informal.

Unorthodox, unbound, unchained, untied.

On the loose, liberated, set free from parental control or any ruling habit, self-governed, self-sufficient, self-contained, unrestrained, uninhibited, a free-thinker.

An admirer of freedom, independence, and opportunities.

Fascinating, enthralling, bewitching, provocative, titillating, mesmerizing, hypnotized, spellbound, in a trance.

One Who Desires ...

To be free so he can do what he wants to do and when he wants to do something.

To freelance his work or do temporary (part-time) jobs, or to be his own boss (stemming from a desire to be independent, free and to work when he feels like it).

To hear about the latest news or craze.

The latest thing, the rage, the fad, place or thing.

To let his hair down and be himself; the new, modern or novel because it is appealing and fascinating ... this may be a new person, job, hobby or a new way of doing things; to leave, withdraw, abandon and part from settled, recognized and standard conventions, usages and habits.

To improve self.

Change, whether it is a move, a new job, a new hairstyle, a dress, a new love or cosmetic surgery.

To spring surprises on others.

One Who Can ...

Interpret individual personalities and character with accuracy (intuitively or through psychology or astrology ... scientifi-cally reached with the latter two subjects).

See through, note or discover rapidly how others respond to ad-vice, proposals, ideas, offers and recommendations.

Accommodate, adjust and reconcile what he sees, perceives, dis-covers or detects.

Do the unprecedented, uncustomary, unheard of or invent, utilize and create something unusual.

Contrive, plan, design and think up odd, out-of-the-ordinary and uncommon plans, notions or views and fresh, novel and new-fangled routines, formulas, techniques, short cuts or ways and means.

Become involved in new enterprises, endeavors, ventures, tasks, moves, adventures, business, work, projects, affairs or pursuits.

Stand on his own two feet.

Do things instantaneously without a moment's notice with no
previous preparation or forethought.

Arise and meet emergencies.

Move forward and advance to new areas.

Affect, impress, sway, control, motivate and persuade others;
talk and express his individuality so powerfully and magneti-
cally that he attracts others and carries them off their feet.

Be paralyzed with delight by another.

Feel the sky's the limit.

Feel in the mood to go on an escapade or a lark.

Revolt against authority (on the harmonious side of Uranus he
has a better chance of getting by with it than he does on the
discordant side of Uranus).

One Who Has . . .

Thoughts and theories that are advanced, up to date, modern and
sometimes too far ahead of the times.

Ideas, plots, aims, outlines, intentions, projects, arrangements,
deals, proposals or strategies suddenly changed without prior
notification (the sudden changes which occur can be through
a person and may be in reverse of his hopes, wishes or anticipations but in some manner it may be beneficial).

A quirk, idiosyncracy.

A passing fancy.

A fascination.

A momentary crush.

A fling.

A great power of attracting and winning.

Pull or charm and can captivate another so the other person is
hypnotized, magnetized and spellbound.

An unprepared and extremely forcible separation from someone
or the rendering asunder of some kind (it is for the best even
though he may be in shock).

One May Attract . . .

New enterprises, people, friendships, changes, ventures or paths; sudden and unanticipated changes, alterations, deviations, diversions, transitions and/or revisions (these turnabouts or reversals are for one's betterment).

Unlooked-for, surprising and from out of left field events, experiences, incidents, conditions, developments and situations.

Others who catch him off guard.

People he hasn't seen in a long time (they show up or pop into the life like a bolt of lightning).

One May Attract the Following Type of Incident . . .

Meet a new person who has her spellbound. This could be an intense and firm affection where she feels paralyzed to stop it. This new person may have an excessively forceful, conspicuous and noticeable power, effect, sway and control over her. She may be guided into all sorts of actions and behavior that she usually would not consider or think of. Most likely this attraction will not last. Once the spell is broken and the person is out of her life she will have a broader, more extensive, far-ranging, sweeping slant and outlook. She will have gained from this relationship with costly, invaluable and worthwhile discernments and perceptions. Her conscious and subconscious mind will have grown, developed and been improved and will be on a high level. She may feel as if her life had been cut in half, as though one phase or part of her life has concluded. The following phase is one of blossoming, unfolding and spreading herself to new views, outlooks and prospects. She may feel like a new person living a new life.

Type of People . . .

One who uses the actions and traits listed under the harmonious side of Uranus, or whose hobby and/or work deals with anything listed under the harmonious side of Uranus.

Foreigner, alien, one who is a different nationality than oneself.

Gypsies, vagabonds, bohemians.

One Whose Hobby and/or Work Deals With . . .

Anything listed under the harmonious side of Uranus.

Astrology, occultism, hypnotism.

Research.

Electronics, computers, loudspeakers, microphones.

Wiring, telephone wires, electricity.

Appliances, gadgets and equipment where electricity is used (scanner, copy machine, electric typewriter), modern devices where mechanics are involved.

Automobiles, space ships, boats and jets (the wiring, electricity or electronic part).

Inventions, novelties, innovations.

New products, processes, equipment or new plants.

Up-to-date products.

Modern furniture or equipment.

New fads, new slant or twist on something, development of new and improved strains (breeding in animals and plants).

Following the exact principles and laws of science.

New information.

New clothes, jewelry, hairstyles.

Newfangled, recent, just out, fresh images, thoughts, views, notions or brain storms regarding concepts, theories, surmises, encounters, finds, detections, discoveries, discernments or perceptions.

Something that is sole and exclusive.

Originality.

Change, reform, strikes.

Anything considered avant-garde.

Discordant Uranus

One Who . . .

Abandons, forsakes, quits and drops out of the normal, accepted and customary things of life to do his own thing and is unconcerned and disinterested in other people's thoughts, reactions and opinions.

Holds in his mind disfavored, disliked and disesteemed ideas, opinions, concepts and impressions.

Gratifies his desires and tastes by using odd, unusual, uncommon and outlandish manners and modes of talking (tone, accent, delivery or words).

Tries to alter, amend and vary current ways and means in an extreme and fanatical manner.

Makes and abides by his own rules, discipline and system.

Desires to freelance.

Couldn't care less what others think of him.

Becomes restless with normal and orthodox conventions and proprieties or with popular, current and prevalent thoughts and the so-called establishment.

Revolts, disobeys and rises against authority or rebels against anything that displeases him.

Balks and refuses to go along with the crowd or others.

Can't seem to make plans because his plans are always being turned upside-down.

Rushes, hurries and goes helter-skelter through life instead of in a slower, more relaxed manner.

Quits, gets fired or gets rid of others in a very quick and unprepared-for manner; changes his sex through an operation (also Mars . . . the operation; Uranus is the change, the new person, the unusual) and has ill effects . . . problems arise either of a mental or physical nature.

One Who Is . . .

Evicted, stranded or abandoned.

Too independent.

Unruly, irresponsible, disinterested and unconcerned about customs, proprieties, normal and expected ways or things.

High-strung, tense, edgy, twitchy, jumpy, jittery.

Uneasy, overwrought, shaky.

Unsynchronized, uncoordinated.

Not in tune with self or others.

Mentally distracted, mixed up and disorientated.

Always in motion, roving, unsettled or astir.

Erratic, unreliable, undependable, unsure, indefinite.

Negligent, thoughtless.

Unthinking, inadvertent, neglectful and unmindful of others; inconstant.

Abrupt, curt, brusque.

Sloppy (because he is in too much of a hurry and doesn't want to take the time to place things in order or to do things carefully).

Rebels against those in power.

In exile, a displaced person, cast out and rejected by others, excluded from fellowship.

Strange, odd, bizarre, freakish, abnormal, peculiar, unaccepted or unapproved by others.

Eccentric, unusual, informal, irregular and uncommon in clothing worn, or in pursuits, responses, conduct, behavior, undertakings, concepts, ideas, thoughts or views.

Opposed and adverse to the actions and opinions of others.

Difficult, complex and perplexing to size up, form an opinion on, estimate or to decide (the preceding also may be applied to a business or any activity).

Quizzical.

Overly distant, far-off and ahead of the moment, era, period of time, future or century.

One Who Has . . .

Curious, uncommon, phenomenal, strange, uncanny and unusual adventures, escapades, ordeals, trials or tribulations.

Rare, off the beaten path, out of the ordinary and unheard of experiences or ideas.

Fresh, avant-garde, unique and unattempted ideas or inventions.

Experimental and untested ideas, theories or inventions.

Unheard of plans or projects.

Experiences, events or happenings occur absent of some notice, omen, alarm, tip-off or prediction.

Unanticipated incidents that may bring deviations from his plans . . . and the projects may suddenly not turn out, or fail to materialize at the very end or in the concluding stage.

Previously made plans proceed and progress inaccurately, incorrectly and improperly.

Cancellations (other people cancel on him or he cancels on others).

A bomb drop from out of the blue (the bomb may be through shocking words spoken by another or from an actual ignited bomb).

His aspirations, desires, aims and goals turned upside-down.

Complicated, detailed and computed designs, plans or proposals are disturbed, toppled or overturned in a jiffy, flash or moment; things unexpectedly in an upheaval or commotion.

Things unfold in an unlooked-for and surprising manner.

To declare bankruptcy.

Unexpected reversals.

His regular pattern of arrangement and distribution disrupted.

All sorts of disruptions.

Changes or transformations.

Swift, impulsive, impetuous and foolish ideas (usually way-out).

His room or abode appears like a tornado had struck.

A friend, loved one, a member of the family, coworker or employee who suddenly vanishes and leaves no trace of his whereabouts and becomes a missing person; abandoned his home, child, family or another and has disappeared.

A frenzied and uncontrollable rendering asunder of things.

Incidents and occurrences generally unapprehended, unexplained

and unascertained may create a puzzle or jolt, but there is
benefit and gain denoted, implied or disclosed in a particular
course, line or direction.

In one area he may profit and in another area he may lose, or be
in an unfavorable or an inadvisable situation.

A termination of something, usually resulting in a new beginning.

Temporary work, part-time work.

A job cease, end or discontinued . . . he may quit, be fired, walk
out, be laid off or the company is being transferred to another
locale.

Radical political convictions or any convictions that are way-out.

One May Attract . . .

Mutiny, strikes, disrupted aims, schemes, maneuvers, arrangements, deals, inconveniences, perplexities or dilemmas.

Matters that may be unsettled, unwarned and unadvised . . . these
upsets may lead to being jarred, shocked and stunned; affairs,
concerns or interests may become snarled, confusing or
baffling.

Conditions or situations may be in a disorganized or confused
state; alienations, estrangements, reconciliations, disputes,
disagreements, controversies, a falling out with others, breaks
or surprise partings.

Mishaps, haphazards or accidents (these matters may be attended
by injury, damage or loss . . . and may come through other
people).

A short circuit in, or have the following get out of order: complex machines, implements, tools, wiring, appliances, automobiles or anything that uses an electric current or is power
driven by a motor.

One May Attract the Following Type of Incident . . .

A romance, flirtation, love affair or amour that is short-lived,
non-enduring and dissolves; it does not continue for any
length of time. The person in love believes it will endure for-

ever. She may be affected, impressed and emotionally aroused to such a point that her life is uprooted and she does things she normally wouldn't do. The new person that came into the life may have her completely mesmerized. She may feel an unexpected, impulsive and forceful affection and devotion for this new person. This new person may have a regrettable, deplorable, adverse and catastrophic power, hold, control, dominance and effect over her. She may have excessive, unreasonable, unsuitable and wrong assurance, trust, faith and certainty in the new person. This new person may have an enormous and/or injurious influence over her. It may be to such an extent that the new person can manipulate her the way he desires. She may not be aware of what is occurring because she is completely hypnotized by him. Her life is topsy-turvy and she does not realize all the events which are transpiring. Soon there is an unexpected, swift and abrupt parting, or the new person stays at a distance which keeps her in puzzlement as to why. They may reconcile and temporarily go back together or they may be back and forth with each other for a long period of time.

Many times after one has broken with one person, one is attracted to a new person, or someone who is an old flame returns, or one may see an old friend. If it is a new love coming into the life, one may be just as fascinated and enthralled as with the last one.

Note: As long as the aspect is in, one can continue with one person after another . . . a love them or leave them attitude, and an in-and-out-of-love situation where there is always a replacement. When people are separated and go back together and part again . . . this separation period and reconciling will depend upon how long the aspect is in both charts, or, in some cases, one chart. For example, if two people are married to each other and the one has a discordant aspect with Uranus involving the seventh house (marriage) and the major progressed aspect is a parallel which sets off a natal discordant aspect, the aspect may be in for years; therefore, the breaking

up and going back together could go on for years . . . as long
as the aspect is within a one degree orb.

Type of People . . .

One who uses the actions and traits listed under the harmonious
side of Uranus negatively; and/or who uses the actions and
traits listed under the discordant side of Uranus. Also one
whose hobby and/or work deals with anything listed under
the harmonious or discordant side of Uranus; perverse, sexual
deviates or degenerates, homosexuals, beatniks, hippies,
gypsies; vagabonds; bohemians.

One Whose Hobby and/or Work Deals With . . .

Anything listed under the harmonious or discordant side of Uranus.

Harmonious Neptune

One Who . . .

Sets decoys, lays traps or plays tricks (the police use decoys and
lay traps, but this may be performed by anyone for any purpose).

Becomes entangled, occupied and absorbed in impersonations,
masquerades, pretenses or concealments.

Vamps, enraptures, tantalizes, teases, hooks, induces, ensnares,
baits, leads on, lures or gives the come-on to others.

Charms, beckons and interests people and as a result attracts
good into his life with a small amount of exertion, energy,
toil or labor.

Obtains, acquires and wins astonishing advantages and profits
(he can accomplish plenty if he endorses, supports or upholds
these activities by performing, executing and responding to
them with action).

Gives up something he has, or wants, for the good of others . . .
he denies himself for a cause.

Thinks he has impending, menacing, looming, overhanging and
foreboding catastrophies, disasters or misfortune. (This may
produce, induce or provoke an immense and boundless anxi-

ety, qualm, dread or alarm which makes him feel panic-stricken. When the supposed disasters approach they are not as bad as he had imagined because nothing much comes of them.)

Believes the unreal is attractive.

Believes reality is mental and sees things as they should be instead of how they are.

Accepts fancied things as fact.

Pretends, play acts with emotion.

Walks or treads on air.

Unfailingly and unremittingly hunts, quests and explores everywhere for his supreme standard of perfection (this may be an ideal person or belief or life).

Perceives and feels there exists a more perfect, absolute, improved, preferable and superior condition or circumstance than what he has thus far found (these situations, if found, may be applied, employed or utilized as continuous goals; that is, if once demonstrated, verified, tested or proved they are rational, sensible, sane and usable).

Seeks truth through contemplation of things beyond the range of sense perception and evidential reasoning.

Looks for, quests and searches past the bodily, material and corporal for contentment, fulfillment, gratification, peace of mind, serenity and appeasement.

Sees and communicates with spirits, ghosts, spooks with good results.

Sees mirages and finds them exciting.

Yearns, longs, pines and hankers for heavenly conditions.

Falls or goes into raptures.

Wallows in enraptured ecstasy.

Dreams of riches.

Lives in the world of fantasy.

Gives reign to his imagination and allows it to run wild by picturing things that are non-existent, illusory, fancied, preposterous, cloud-built and similar to a castle in the air (he enjoys having his head up in the billowing clouds).

One Who Is . . .

Exotic.

Glamorous.

Theatrical.

Aesthetic.

Creative.

Poetic.

Romantic.

Vivid, picturesque.

Mysterious, elusive, unexplainable, exciting and baffling.

Dedicated.

Engaging.

Winsome.

Titillating, provocative, alluring, ravishing, fetching, a siren, a femme fatale, appealing, seductive, a tempter, an enchantress, inviting, intriguing, sensuous.

Touchy, sensitive, sentimental, warm, sympathetic.

Susceptible, suggestible or easily influenced, vicarious.

Responsive and susceptible to supernatural, telepathic, extrasensory perception or clairvoyant powers, force and energy.

Psychic.

Encouraged, reassured, moved, induced, prompted and motivated by invisible powers and energies.

In dreamland, fairyland, wonderland, living in the imaginary world.

Starry-eyed, dewey-eyed.

Looking for the pot of gold at the end of the rainbow.

In reverie, idealistic.

Selfless, compassionate and shows sorrow for the suffering of others.

Impractical, forgetful, absentminded and unable to retain things in the memory.

Inclined to confide in, trust and have faith in, place reliance on, depend on and swear by others.

Confidential, private.

Interested in the occult.

One Who Desires . . .

To escape from a person, people, a situation, the environment, the house, life or from everyday mundane affairs or from actuality.

To be a recluse, to keep apart from others or to keep aloof.

Better things in the environment and whatever he takes up or learns he may want to adopt as part of his life (if these things are not too way-out, or impractical, they may, forever, become part of his pattern for living).

To gain or obtain his inner-most enchantment, pleasure, rapture or contentment from existing in his own invented, created, fabricated, fanciful, mythical and make-believe sphere or utopian universe (in this world he can let his imagination wander, spin images and fantasies . . . all is unreal in this world that he has created and he doesn't want to wake up to reality).

One Who Can . . .

Show and feel pity for others.

Be secretive.

Cover up and camouflage.

Hide objects and later can't remember where they are.

Retire.

Go into a trance and receive revelations or illuminations.

Communicate with the dead.

Arouse the curiosity of others.

Be mystical.

Be delusively charming.

Be captivating, enchanting, mystical.

Envision, picture and imagine an invention, production or idea from beginning to end, and if he were to perform, pursue or act on it, he would be able to use an inconceivable, incredible and fantastic smoothness, competence and efficiency in its accomplishment.

Get others to become fascinated, enthralled, absorbed, concerned, perked up and engrossed in his projects, propositions, deals, schemes or business affairs (this is accomplished through his ability to communicate with ebullience, inspiration and gentle persuasive methods employed with a slow, deliberate, determined and irresistible force).

One Who Has . . .

A come-hither look.

A yen for some person or object.

A feeling of bliss.

Romantic or utopian dreams.

Happy illusions.

Visions in his sleep.

Desirous, wistful and wantful but *unreal* daydreams.

Dreams of a world where everyone and everything is beautiful.

A desire for perfection.

Vapors, smoke and bubbles getting into his mind's eye.

Inspiration, castle-building and fantasy enhanced, magnified, exaggerated and enlarged to enormous portions.

A love potion to give to another.

Flights of fancy.

A lively, constructive, poetic or reproductive imagination.

Elevated, exalted or immodest emotion, sensitivity, sentimentality.

A deep feeling of sharing the suffering of another with an inclination to give aid, support or to show mercy.

Illuminations.

Psychic experiences.

A memory gap.

Something on the tip of his tongue and the idea escapes him or
fades away.

Mental energy to promote on an immense and enormous level.

The ability to ballyhoo so he can further his aims.

Ideas or concepts of effortless, simple and carefree affluence, opulence and riches devoid of too much work.

Indefinite, unclear and uncertain cravings, desires and
hankerings.

One Who Feels . . .

Like becoming involved in only spiritual things and wants to get
away from the hum-drum of everyday living because he feels
that there are better things in a spiritual world than what there
is in the world of reality.

Useful work and undertakings are not important. Only the more
excellent, exceptional and superior than material things are
important.

That existence is invaluable and priceless only if he is effectuat-
ing ethereal and other-worldly elevation, improvement, development and growth.

Like retiring, being a recluse, dreaming and being peaceful.

That his only way to progress in a spiritual world is to withdraw
from life and people and go into this other world where he
can meditate and have visions, esp experiences and illuminations (this is a temporary feeling while the aspect is within a
one degree orb and it does have some beneficial results).

One May Attract . . .

Real or imagined plots, plans and tactics that bring fast, speedy
and rapid money, wealth and affluence.

Someone who commits himself, pledges his word, makes a vow,
gives his word of honor, guarantees or commits himself to a
plan, project or undertaking which may result in ten percent
of what was promised or agreed upon.

Broken promises and slight disappointments with people who
broke them or one may make the promises to others and later,

break them (this aspect can occur on the discordant side of Neptune; however, on the harmonious side of Neptune, one isn't as upset and everything happens for the best of all concerned).

One May Attract the Following Type of Incident . . .

A request for love may be made to one's softer side which arouses the love nature. One wants to hold hands, be wined and dined by candlelight and listen to soft melodious music . . . everything is rosy, poetic and romantic. One may be inspired with unreasonable passion or attraction. The affinity with another may make one feel amorous and infatuated. One idolizes the loved one by giving the person imaginary attributes that do not exist. One's delicate, sensitive, more complex, entangled and involved sentiments, sensibilities and feelings may be aroused to a foolish degree. Extravagant feelings of ecstasy and rapture build so the mental rapport becomes more important than the physical attraction. One believes that this is his ideal love (it may be while the aspect is in orb). The relationship may not last. There may be an odd, slow and little by little degrees of detachments or partings. Gradually one is separated from the person or may willingly (on his part) and without force deliberately disown, reject, repudiate, withdraw and give the person up.

Type of People . . .

One who uses the actions and traits listed under the harmonious side of Neptune, or whose hobby and/or work deals with anything listed under the harmonious side of Neptune.

One who worships male movie stars or popular singers.

Actor, actress, playwright (also Mercury; Neptune is the ability to dramatize), impressionist; impersonator,

Public relations person (Neptune is the promoting part), promoter.

One Whose Hobby and/or Work Deals With . . .

Anything listed under the harmonious side of Neptune.

Gas, oil, petroleum.

The handling of poisons, insecticides.

Drugs, pills, patent medicines, pharmacies, the field of medicine (exploring part), anesthesia, ether.

Mold, mildew, fungus, mushrooms, truffles.

Pearls.

Swimming, floating on a raft or on top of the water, drowning (a lifeguard).

Camouflage.

Laying traps or decoys (police).

Air conditioning.

Sea cruises.

Navigation.

Jets, airplanes, seaplanes, aviation, spacecraft, flying, gliding (airplanes or high in the imagination), balloons, dirigibles, parachuting.

Mediums, mysticism.

Foam rubber.

The stock market (also fifth house).

Booms (oil, gold, stock), bonanzas.

Retirement.

Pastimes, amusements.

Excursions, picnics, vacations, outings, holidays, fiestas.

Resting and taking life easy by doing nothing other than day-dreaming or watching movies or television.

Schemes where many people may share in the profit.

Incorporation schemes (also may be Pluto and Saturn).

Painting (also Venus; Neptune is the figment of the imagination, mental image and visualization part), art, collage, surrealistic or abstract painting.

Photography, film, video, microfilm, cinema, movies, movie industry, movies made for television (also Pluto).

The stage, theatre, theatrical productions.

Show business, entertainment.

Music (the creative and dramatic part).

Dramatic work such as acting, kabuki, make-believe, plays, skits, drama, tragedy (also Saturn).

Opera, pantomime; burlesque; pageant.

Monologue, dialogue, comedy, revues; soap opera (also Pluto), variety shows (also Moon); reviews (a show), vaudeville, concerts.

Striking and fabulous musical or dramatic pieces, often with fantastic settings and characterized by eccentricity, wildness or splendor in costumes and settings with enormous casts.

Spectacular extravaganzas.

Sequins, glitter, headpieces trimmed with furs and chiffon material (also Venus; Neptune is the dramatic effect and creative imagination part).

Elaborate hats done on a large and dramatic scale.

Designing clothes, costumes, homes.

Fairyland, Disneyland.

Masquerade parties (also Venus, the party part . . . Neptune is the masquerade part)

Make-up (also Venus, the cosmetic part . . . Neptune is the disguise and covering up as well as the creative part).

Fiction writing (stories, dramas, fables, myths, inventive and unreal stories).

Poetry.

Prolific and imaginative writing.

Creative areas where one romanticizes, glamorizes, stages or shows and presents, one's feelings, sentiments and sensibilities in some manner, fashion, mode, method or shape.

Conversations, discussions, chitchat and idle talk performed in a dramatic manner.

Promoting (attempting to sell or popularize by advertising or by securing financial support).

Discordant Neptune

One Who . . .

Tackles, starts on, accepts and undertakes or assumes new and novel undertakings that later prove to be worthless, wasted, futile, profitless or unproductive.

Miscolors, falsifies, misstates, under or overstates his aims, plans, business or personal affairs.

Practices the art of swindling, puts on a false front.

Confides in, trusts, accredits, has faith in, counts on, swears by and banks on others and in return he is fooled or deceived.

Must safeguard and screen himself against being impressionable, affected, swayed, inspired and controlled by a person who may attempt to solicit, ask, request and appeal to his sense of pity, empathy or warmheartedness (this person may please, delight, enchant and entice him into unusable and inapplicable routes or tracks of thinking, decision making or reasoning).

Stalls.

Abandons others in a crisis.

Goes incognito, wears a mask.

Puts on a hoax, plans booby traps, ensnares others, cheats (with games or on a loved one).

Believes and/ or imagines the loved one is cheating or that someone is cheating him in a game.

Makes mountains out of molehills.

Puts on an act or stretches the truth, deviates from the truth, enlarges upon the truth.

Overstates and overemphasizes, talks big, talks in superlatives.

Falls hook, line and sinker for a person or what another says.

Plays possum, poses as something he is not.

Exists and lives life with extraordinary concealment of true feelings or intentions under the pretense of being what he is not.

Drifts through life never amounting to anything.

Builds castles in the air.

Exists in a sphere or circle of his creation, flight and fancy.

Depicts, envisions, pictures, visualizes, invents, makes up, fabricates and sees things that are not real or in being.

Believes reality is mental.

Sees things as they should be instead of how they actually are.

Strays, escapes, takes flight and lives in a secluded dream world, fantasy and unreality.

Flies high on a cloud and doesn't want to come down as he enjoys being lost in his own wish-fulfilled world.

Drowns (in an ocean, lake, swimming pool, bathtub, well).

Goes down under in quicksand.

Sinks into oblivion.

Sees pink elephants, spirits, ghosts or a mirage and is upset as a result.

Dislikes being aroused or brought back to truth, reality, actuality or plain facts.

Is too responsive, impressionable or susceptible to the plots and plans of others.

Doesn't like to work nine to five hours.

Disfavors rules, codes, regulations, timetables, schedules and physical or manual labor.

One Who Is . . .

Overly demonstrative, moving, stirring.

Overly impractical and dreams too much about idealistic ideas.

Too sacrificing and gives up too much for the good of others.

Unselfish; high from his own thinking or from pills, drugs, pot or booze.

In a delirium, in a daze, in a coma, out of his mind, in limbo, dizzy, giddy, fainting.

Too lenient, too forgiving, overly warm-hearted, overly merciful.

Too imaginary, too utopic.

Overly romantic.

Readily bamboozled, naive, gullible, too trusting, unrealistic, accepts fancied things as fact.

A sitting duck, pigeon, duped or an easy mark.

Searching for departures from the mind and from the severe restraining walls of actuality, fact and reality.

Preoccupied and engrossed in musing and dreaming thoughts that appear authentic, factual and genuine but that are false, imaginary and nonexistent.

Mentally escaping from reality.

Nebulous, unclear, indistinct, faint, lost in a fog and does not know which way to turn, misty.

Mysterious, eerie, bizarre, magical, wacky, crazy, foolish.

Ruled by ideas or desires to the point of having a mania or feeling of being haunted, beset or harassed by another.

Full of baloney, full of hooey and nonsense.

A phony, humbug, sham, a fraud.

Dishonest, backhanded, not genuine, a smooth talker, a charmer, insincere, deceptive, tricky, fraudulent.

All talk, no action, merely show.

A wind bag who boasts to impress people and does not put words into action . . . therefore, there are no results of what was promised.

Too stagy, showy, theatrical.

Incorrect, untrue, fictitious, perfidious, disloyal, faithless, shiftless, slothful.

One Who Desires . . .

To plot, plan and devise things with the suggestion or idea of using trickery on others.

To disguise, hide, cover-up, obliterate, cloak, mask and withhold things.

Concealed, indistinct and doesn't want fame or attention drawn to him.

To retire, depart, keep aloof and apart from clique, companionship, comradeship, people in general or communities.

To withdraw, abandon or forsake the world by being remote, a recluse or leading a retired life.

To be lazy, to loaf and sit around doing nothing except day-dreaming.

Too much perfection in the world or from people.

To play games with others (from an intriguing, love of mystery viewpoint).

One Who Can . . .

Magnify, overdo, amplify, overestimate, overstate, stretch a point, exaggerate, concoct tall or trumped-up stories.

Tell fairy tales, the half-truth, white lies, a pack of lies, whoppers.

Lie like a trooper, warp, embellish, embroider, fib, fabricate and invent falsehoods.

Falsify records, documents or any object of truth.

Misshape, garble, misrepresent, twist and control actuality, data and circumstances, disguise topics, problems or questions by indefinite, unclear and uncertain remarks or means.

Delude, dupe, fool and be dishonest with self or others.

Be false.

Put something over on someone, pull another's leg, pull the wool over another's eye.

Shortchange others, chisel, fudge, finagle, sell one a bill of goods, cheat, swindle, fleece others, bluff, fake.

Impersonate, pretend, enact, pose, masquerade, simulate, feign or disguise himself by playing a part, making believe or pretending that which is not real.

Imitate falsely an object or person.

Pretend to knowledge not possessed.

Buy, fix, corrupt, give money or other reward offered as an inducement to betray or violate a trust.

Be secretive (to hide wrongdoings).

Be readily influenced, persuaded, controlled, deceived, deluded, tricked, deceived, misguided, misinformed, led astray or taken in.

Win and acquire fulfillment, contentment, delight, gratification, peace of mind, appeasement, self-satisfaction and serenity in his world of make believe.

Do too much romanticizing.

Show too much pity and sharing of the suffering and sorrowing of others.

One Who Has . . .

Towering and lofty prospects, anticipations, views or presumptions without applying toil or hard labor . . . instead the person plots, plans and uses tactics which can bring fast, speedy and rapid money, wealth and affluence; grandiose ideas.

A pipe dream.

Stardust swept into his eyes.

Unrealized hopes.

Useless and impractical desires.

Immaterial dreams.

Impressions, inspirations and thoughts that are towering, vast, enormous and stupendous . . . they are in connection with, or in respect to, plans, propositions, aims or work that are too way-out from what can actually be accomplished . . . therefore, these undertakings usually fall through ... they are like bubbles floating around in the air ready to land on anyone who is gullible enough to reach out and grab these deals or schemes offered.

A wrong slant, outlook or angle.

Self-deception.

Degrading actions.

Inflated ideas.

A false air, illusions of grandeur.

Paranoia (a non-degenerative, limited, usually chronic psychosis characterized by delusions of persecution or of grandeur, strenuously defended by the afflicted person with apparent logic and reason).

A psychosis.

Nightmares.

A mania.

The imagined or real plight of being assailed and dominated by an evil spirit.

Delusions.

Amnesia.

A blackout (from alcohol, drugs or mental reasons).

Supernatural ailments or upsets.

An empty and blank mind, can't think of concrete things.

Difficulty in receiving a psychic reading but can give one to another with some accuracy.

One Who Feels . . .

Like he is on a magic carpet.

Overly colorless, bored, mediocre and too ordinary. Therefore, he may desire something that will inspire, provoke, arouse, stimulate or excite him; something that is lurid and sensational. Whether he takes to drugs, popping pills or drinking liquor or any other crazy notion, he can attract all sorts of problems with his health, daily living and people.

One May Attract . . .

A hoax, be victimized or victimize others.

Propositions that are misrepresented.

Fictional, mistaken, inaccurate and unsound impressions, notions, views, concepts.

Erroneous, unethical and improper notions or inklings.

A promoter who organizes and fosters a new company or deal (which will probably fall through).

Willful and deliberate plots or plans that can have made-up benefits and favors. These propositions are uncommonly and remarkably alluring, appealing, inviting, tempting and intriguing. When understood and perceived in actual existence, fact or truth, they are negative and not very large or notable. They are upgraded, elevated and contain pure ballyhoo concepts, deals, schemes or arrangements. They most likely will fizzle, abort, flop, peter out, collapse, flunk, fold, crash, go up in smoke, be in vain, run aground, fall short of what is promised or what one imagines is going to take place.

The desire for narcotics (cocaine, morphine, opium, heroin, mescaline), drugs, pot (marijuana, tea, hashish), hallucinogens, pills (speed, amphetamines, pep, phenobarbitals, sleeping), alcohol, liquor (also Mars, the stimulant part; Neptune is the beverage and escapism part).

Food poisoning or any poison invading the body.

Difficulty with eliminating poisons from the body.

Germs, bacteria, microbes, parasites.

Wax in the ears (one imagines that he has lost his hearing).

Illnesses that are difficult to diagnose (sixth house also involved).

One May Attract the Following Type of Incident . . .

With a loved one you are infatuated and in ecstasy (see the harmonious side of Neptune under this same heading, because the same feelings can be felt under the discordant side of Neptune).

One gives the loved one imaginary attributes that do not exist. One sees the person as one *wants* to see the person, not as the person is in reality. An illumination gradually takes place. One may not like what one sees. The person may descend (in one's eyes) from up high and depreciate into unworthiness. One had admired this person with worshipful eyes and now the eyes are opened. One looks around and has a letdown, a disenchantment, disillusionment and great disappointment. One realizes how his imagination had run away with him. One may willingly and freely disown, disavow, give up and relinquish the loved one because the pedestal has fallen and one does not feel like picking up the broken pieces.

Type of People . . .

One who uses the actions and traits listed under the harmonious side of Neptune negatively and/or who uses the actions and traits listed under the discordant side of Neptune.

One whose hobby and/or work deals with anything listed under the harmonious or discordant side of Neptune.

A con-artist, forger, counterfeiter, imposter, charlatan, fortune teller, quack, an impersonator (who passes himself off as something he is not).

A fanatic, lunatic, demented.

A nut, crackpot, screwball.

A hobo, beggar, parasite; tramp.

Alcoholic, drug addict.

Psychopath, one who has psychosomatic illnesses, hypochondriac.

Freak (also Uranus; Neptune is the bizarre as well as the person who is disappointed with the way he is).

Lady-killer, heartbreaker, ladies' man, woman chaser.

Philanderer; rolling stone, floater, drifter; beachcomber (shiftless person who lives and hangs around the beaches in search of something in his life and works just enough to exist), playboy (who wastes time and money on amusement).

A woman of easy virtue, call girl, courtesan, prostitute, hooker, streetwalker, hustler, mistress, kept man or kept woman (all living expenses paid in return for sex).

Gigolo, roue, Lothario, Casanova, Don Juan, procurer or procuress, pimp, madam.

Narcotics pusher.

Nymphomaniac.

Debauched, decadent, jaded.

All classes of sexual deviates, transvestite, necrophiliac, fetishist, masochist (mental or physical . . . also Saturn), sadist (also Pluto), sadomasochist (also Saturn and Pluto), voyeur (also Saturn). Note: Sexual deviations are mapped by the fifth house and other factors. These are listed under Neptune for research purposes. Neptune is involved in any form of deviation, especially those where the mind escapes from reality. The chart alone does not map perversion. One must know the conditioning and environment of the native and the case history. One should use caution in making definite statements in this area.

One Whose Hobby and/or Work Deals With . . .

Anything listed under the harmonious or discordant side of Neptune.

Psychedelic attractions.

Fake paintings, artificial objects (like flowers), plastic.

Fog, mist, aerosol sprays (hair sprays, perfume, cleaners, etc.).

Harmonious Pluto

One Who . . .

Believes in, and takes part in, brotherhood.

Cultivates and advances deserving and meritorious causes, charities or foundations.

Enters into and partakes in crusades, expeditions, actions, or in a series of meetings, speeches, lectures or syndications (these activities are for a meriting group, usually a minority class of people).

Enjoys helping human beings in general or the community in its totality, feels like doing good for humanity, feels like serving and benefitting all creation . . . the universe, cosmos and the whole wide world.

Feels his soul is in rapport and tuned in to others (it may be one person he feels tuned in to or a group).

Scatters and broadcasts doctrines and principles in printed matter and delivers speeches for purpose of promoting a cause that is for the good of society.

Plans things on a national or international basis.

Does teamwork and coordinates with those around him.

Asserts, demands, requires and requests things of others (done in a nice way).

Persuades or is persuaded by another in a reputable manner.

Is persistent and doesn't give up until he has accomplished his goal (done in a nice manner).

Forms clubs, fraternizes, flocks (like a herd) with others.

Lives in a boarding house or owns one, lives with others (home for the aged, sanitarium).

Merges, fuses, blends or incorporates in business.

Does business on a shoestring basis.

Serves one person after another (in a store, or a doctor who sees one patient after another).

Waits on crowds (waiter, waitress, sales clerk).

Receives grants from foundations.

Performs white magic.

Senses he is compelled to do things (he may be impressed by an unseen force and feels he *must do* what *he must do* . . . he is being favorably impressed).

Does detective work or anything involving crime, criminals, bootlegging, hijacking or kidnaping.

Adds on an addition to an office, home, restaurant or any structure that is in existence.

Owns or possesses more than one of some material object (office, business establishment, home, apartment, piece of stock, shares, coffee pot, etc.).

One Who . . .

Entangled, enveloped and occupied with clusters and assemblages of people who are involved in active pursuits, movements or vocations which are of similar interests.

In agreement, assists, aids, lends a hand, shares and takes part with groups.

Prominently and essentially linked with action of different types and varieties.

Involved in common, mutual, combined and shared exertion, toil or labor.

Involved in regimentation (to organize, form into units or groups, arrange, separate and control by strict rules for the betterment of all concerned).

Involved in compulsory rules (like the rules of the road).

Takes part in civil rights or any area where minorities are involved.

Involved in women's rights (Uranus also; Pluto is the group betterment part).

Granted control, power or prestige over others for a beneficial cause for all concerned.

In agreement and accordance with others and can work with them because he is helpful, willing to go along with what is necessary and is compatible with the group.

Involved in experimenting or testing (objects, people, chemistry).

Persistent, tenacious and doesn't give up easily.

Energetic with a subtle force.

Compulsive or forceful (in a nice way which does not upset others).

In sympathy and harmony with others and can sense and understand what others feel.

An exorcist.

Inclined to follow the first impression he feels.

A spiritualist or medium (he communicates and is in touch with unseen beings or individuals).

A specialist in any given field.

A teammate, colleague, collaborator.

Involved in joint operations.

A part of a unit or squad (police or vice).

Involved in group theatre parties (also Neptune = theatre; Venus = parties; Pluto = group; fifth house = amusements; twelfth house = charities; and eighth house = funds raised with other people's money).

A mixer, joiner and always with someone . . . never a loner.

One Who Desires . . .

To do good on behalf of others.

To contribute to another's well-being or to some good cause.

To back up, befriend or aid others to achieve, reach, arrive at and accomplish a shared and useful, profitable and favorable mission, objective, effect and result.

To join forces.

To bring people together.

To unite, associate or band together with others.

To take part in or affiliate with a league or in some relationship with others.

To lessen, decrease, diminish, amend and correct tyranny, despotism, autocracy, burdens of hardships or severity.

Worldwide prosperity and well-being.

Group investment.

To form a pool or put into a common fund.

Mutual funds.

To share in collective, joint and communal funds (money, stock or other certificates, etc., which belong to and are shared by a group).

To take a tour (he is interested in the same things as the other members of the tour; on the harmonious side of Pluto, one enjoys being with groups or going on tours; everyone is helpful and cooperative).

One Who Can . . .

Gain satisfaction when protecting, guarding and supporting the privileges, claims, justice and honor of others (policemen fall into this category).

Disregard, omit or blink at conflicts, strife, dissensions and disagreements and has no individual prejudice but wants to achieve and acquire benefits for an objective purpose, target or mission.

Manage people in a clever way so he can bring a desired effect.

Exercise, employ or utilize his power through compelling, driving, pressing, insisting and enforcing things in the interest of the group.

Handle groups of people; investigate matters, affairs, people and keep statistical records of all transactions, or whatever.

Reveal the misuse of power over others.

Alleviate and lessen misery, anguish, agony and pain in others.

Heal (psychically or otherwise).

Do astral projection (release the astral body from material limitations).

Live with groups of people (communal living), ashram.

One Who Has . . .

An uncommon and well developed perception into the thinking and mental reflections of others.

A close and searching inquiry or examination so he can receive knowledge, news, communication, accounts, reports, data or propaganda by tuning in to unusual, rare, uncommon and unaccustomed invisible energies and powers as a source for the answers he is seeking.

A holy and sacred feeling.

A clique, clan or group which he belongs to.

Car or building pools.

Concessions in amusement centers, theatres, stadiums, etc.

Consultations.

Patients.

A compulsion (an irresistible impulse to act regardless of

the rationality of the motivation).

One May Attract . . .

Anything listed under the harmonious side of Pluto.

Group investments in real estate.

Mergers.

Franchises.

A place that is jam-packed (filled to capacity with crowds).

Type of People . . .

One who uses the actions and traits listed under the harmonious side of Pluto, or whose hobby and/or work deals with anything listed under the harmonious side of Pluto.

Crowds, groups.

Choruses, bands, orchestras, rock or group bands, singers or musicians.

Groupies.

Umpires.

Mediators, arbitrators, negotiators, reconcilers, peacemakers, intercessors.

Astronauts.

Radio chemists.

Physicians, nurses.

Clerks.

Farmers (involved in mass production of food and they plant more than one item).

Treasury Department investigative agent.

Spies, foreign and secret agents (employed by a country for the good of said country).

Those who do undercover and underground work (for the good of a cause).

Federal Bureau of Investigation employee.

Federal Communications Commission employee (enforces a code for the radio and television industry).

Collection agent.

Those who are persistent, helpful and cooperative on the harmonious side of Pluto.

One Whose Hobby and/or Work Deals With . . .

Anything listed under the harmonious side of Pluto.

Business where regimentation or organization is involved.

Controlling the concepts, slants and appraisals of society and the populace.

Protecting others from attacks, intrusions, invasions (the service, police work).

Counterintelligence, counterespionage.

Put in action and to use by exploring the most recent finds, encounters, discoveries, devises, designs or inventions.

Database/processing.

Microchips, microdots.

Atomic energy and tests, atoms.

Chemistry experiments.

Chemicals.

Labs.

Socialized medicine.

Microsurgery.

Foundations.

Spiritual camps or retreats.

The United Nations or any type business or area where others are united for a common and worthwhile cause.

Unions, guilds, federations, leagues.

Syndicates (newspapers, movies, television, department or grocery stores).

Corporations, companies.

Chains, stores, markets

Meetings, conventions.

Mergers.

Bureaus, commissions, committees.

Investigations (by one or a committee).

Medicine (also Neptune; Pluto is the chemical part).

Microwaves.

X-rays.

Lasers.

MRI machines.

Chemotherapy.

Invisible objects (fluorescent objects that are invisible until a fluorescent lamp is flashed upon them is one example. This lamp is frequently used in dance halls so the crowds (Pluto) can leave and re-enter without re-paying).

Jam sessions (meetings at which musicians play).

Recordings, recorders (DVD, CD, MP3, film), radio, video, short-wave radio, cable TV, television, two-way radio.

Assembly lines, mass production of any object or work done by means of mass production techniques.

Things being uniform, in unison and with clockwork precision ... an evenness required in the job or method of doing things, everything is done alike . . . for example, The Rockettes in New York City's Radio City Music Hall are in the same costume and do precision work, or the Playboy Club has the girls dressed alike and on the job they must obey the rules.

Uniforms (waitress, nurse, painter, mechanic, school, etc.).

Clubs (private, public or night clubs where crowds gather).

Organized groups.

Franchises.

Packing (a collection of items or wrapped in a bundle), packaging.

Packing or crowding people closely together as is done in night clubs, restaurants, shows.

The packing business where items may be packed in various ways).

Lines (waiting in one or working where there are lines of people or a police line-up or football line-up).

Licenses, licensing (fashion world).

Prefabricated homes (constructed in advance in quantity . . . standard units or sub-units).

Parcels of land that are later subdivided.

Subdivision.

Tract homes.

Additions to homes or any structure.

Hotels, motels, units, cottages, duplex, apartments, condominiums, co-ops, shopping centers, malls or shopping plazas (any place where there is more than one of something . . . for example, hotels have many rooms that are rented to more than one individual.

Shopping plazas have more than one space which is rented to more than one individual or company).

Religious, spiritual or astrology work (where one is helping and giving aid to another).

Group therapy (used in psychology), healing.

Congregations (those who attend a religious service).

Group tours (walking, car, bus, airplane . . . where people are guided through a city, countryside, museum, church, etc. where the group is banded together and the people have a mutual interest).

Discordant Pluto

One Who . . .

Senses he is compelled to do things (he may be impressed by an unseen force and feels *he must do* what *he must do* . . . he may be unfavorably impressed by the dark forces).

Does not allow anyone to stop any of his desires from expressing (he feels his desires must be accomplished at all costs and he will allow no one to stand in his way of completing them . . . if someone attempts to block them, all hell will break loose and he will employ destructive tactics against the person trying to block his efforts).

Utilizes, employs and exercises his initiative, pep, fortitude, endurance and money or assets to oppose society and people.

Drives, coerces and takes others by force.

Walks over and uses others for his own selfish gain.

Displeases or offends.

Plunders and fleeces the masses.

Collaborates with dubious people who may impede his progress.

Resorts to exploitation.

Takes drastic action and makes drastic changes that may be against his welfare or that of others.

Writes or receives poison pen (hate) letters.

Overhangs, impends, intimidates others or is a menace (Mars also; Pluto is the forceful, persistent and badgering part).

Badgers others.

Incites, provokes, goads or opposes another.

Employs force.

Harasses a person or is the one harassed or threatened.

Plots to make an innocent person look guilty.

Occupies himself in dissension, strife and friction of opposite concern.

Prevails over others with coercive tactics.

Antagonizes others resulting in groups who oppose him.

Plays both ends against the middle, two-faced.

Plays a double game or role.

Takes sides, collaborates, joins forces or unites with others in a common interest which is detrimental to everyone.

Does not feel like cooperating with others but usually rebels if anyone uses insistence upon him; brings into play the most recent and newest finds, or that which is brought to light for the first time to devise, contrive or concoct something which can be used against another for his own self-seeking desires.

May experience plights, inconveniences or trouble with a person who has a supernatural and psychic manipulation, dominance, control, sway or hold over an individual . . . this mastery over him could interfere with, and hinder, his constructive endeavors (a person attracts it because he has a towering amount of opposite, contrary and resistive feelings, impressions and reactions and is sensitive and negative to everything and everyone, including himself).

Breaks and violates rules or regulations (parking and traffic laws or company rules and policies).

Dislikes group tours because he doesn't want to follow rules or to be forced to see what he is not interested in, or to do what he doesn't want to do, or to go somewhere he doesn't want to go . . . he is uncooperative on group tours and may feel that crowds are a source of difficulty.

One Who Is . . .

Persistent to the point that others want to rebel, avoid or to be unavailable.

Relentless, remorseless, pitiless, merciless (also Saturn).

Ruthless.

Sadistic (also Mars and Neptune).

Haunted or harassed by one desire or idea . . . obsessed (also Neptune).

Unfriendly.

Inimical.

Averse.

Antagonistic (also Mars).

Crooked, dishonest, cruel-hearted, a menace, a criminal, sneaky, a troublemaker, harmful, wrong, wicked, evil, damaging, detrimental, deplorable, sinister, hostile, full of hatred.

A dictator, oppressor, controller, ruler, tyrant.

A hellion who causes worry, distress, grief, adversities and molests others.

A rapist or the person who is raped.

Boycotted or does the boycotting.

Blackballed or does the blackballing.

Banished or does the banishing.

Exiled or does the exiling (also Uranus).

Ostracized or does the ostracizing.

Lynched or does the lynching (hanging . . . mob—Pluto—excitement).

Hijacked or does the hijacking.

Kidnaped or does the kidnaping.

Framed or does the framing.

Blackmailed or does the blackmailing.

On a black list or that has a black list.

The one bribed (also Neptune; Pluto is the persuasion and illegal part) or does the bribing.

The one shanghaied (taken away by force) or does the shanghaiing.

The prey, pawn, dupe or easy mark of abductors or kidnappers.

A mass murderer or one who is the victim.

Obsessed by demons.

A mischief (causing harm, injury or damage).

Malicious.

Bewitched.

Charmed by witchcraft into doing bad things.

In slavery, bondage or involuntary servitude (also Neptune; Pluto is the involuntary part).

Involved in segregating others due to racial prejudice.

Involved in extortion, stolen or hot goods, illegal activities, pay-offs, lawbreaking, smuggling, selling illicit liquor.

Involved in running a regular action of gambling, extortion, shakedowns, prostitution or any business which is contrary to the law.

Involved in illegitimate concerns (including children born out of wedlock).

Involved in rackets.

Involved in syndicates (any kind).

One Who Desires ...

To achieve, accomplish, gain, acquire and seek his own personal interests and aims without regard to others.

To hurt others to gain his own selfish wishes.

More and more of an object, money, material possession or person or anything else and he wants it at all costs.

To turn the world upside down . . . to overturn or overthrow, and to demolish and ruin everything which can result in disastrous events.

To isolate himself from crowds, groups or pressures.

One Who Can ...

Organize or form into units or groups and arranges, separates and controls others by strict rules for the ill of others.

Incite and provoke different types of bad, abominable, dreadful misdemeanors, wicked felonies and illegal misdeeds.

Employs unjust ways and means of procedures.

Persuade another in an irreputable manner or is persuaded by another in an irreputable manner.

Instigate or partake in undertakings that are opposed to, or destructive of, human society.

Apply formulas, techniques, ways and means in an upside down reversed manner which is against others.

Scatter and broadcast doctrines and principles in printed matter and deliver speeches for purpose of promoting a cause that can be against society.

Turn one side against the other.

Stir up and instigate friction between sides.

Employ his supernatural or psychic powers for calculated, sordid, self-concerned, self-indulgent and self-interested reasons.

One Who Has . . .

A connection, affiliation, relationship or association with clubs, organizations and/or people of uncertain and dubious caliber, ethics, character or viewpoints.

Deadlines to meet and must meet them by using force and being isolated from others.

An abortion (if it is illegal; something may be illegal in one city or country but not in another . . . read all illegal activities in connection with the place where one resides or visits).

One Who Uses . . .

Pressure, insistence and persistence on others or they use it on him.

Actions, motions, pursuits or vocations where a policy or coercion by intimidation and terror is employed.

Dishonest and unjust arrangements, plans, contracts and concepts.

Excessive, unreasonable, untimely, improper and unsuitable strain, tension, stress, urgency, compulsion or constraint upon self or others.

Force upon self or others; cowardly, furtive, concealed and underhanded techniques, tactics, schemes, strategy and theories.

Calculated, small-minded, sordid, base, self-interested and self-seeking aims, intentions, objectives, ambitions or goals to accomplish his resolution, will, target, mission or ulterior purpose.

His own rules, regulations and laws of action or conduct to make others do as he desires (these actions can be sneaky or obvious).

Intimidation of another.

Rebellion against law and control.

Devious means to eliminate obstacles, regardless of costs or outcome to others and he does not allow those close to him to interfere with his plans or desires.

Black magic, voodoo, witchery, incantations and evil spells.

One May Attract . . .

Vandalism.

Robberies.

Burglaries.

Protests.

Wild-cat or sit-down strikes.

Mobs, masses, street gangs, gangs, and swarms of people and have difficulty with them, or they use force or underhanded tactics.

Extreme, dire and drastic incidents, occurrences and happenings or drastic alterations, amendments, modifications, shifts, deviations, transpositions, diversions, reversals, turnabouts or innovations.

Physical attack or coercion.

Others who gang up on and band together in a common pursuit against him.

Problems with regimentation.

Organized groups or corporations which can result in harassment or problems.

Difficulties with associates or associations.

A problem with cooperation involving group activities, movements and actions . . . the source of difficulty may be in getting others to give or share equally.

A problem of where one is put on the spot, or placed in a discordant situation, or depicted in a negative light or trapped in some incident by an underhanded person; problems with movements, clusters or assemblages of people who are forcible, tough, defiant and averse to him because he is in a different league, alliance or group and does not agree or go along with them.

Type of People . . .

One who uses the actions and traits listed under the harmonious side of Pluto negatively; and/or who uses the actions and traits listed under the discordant side of Pluto.

One whose hobby and/or work deals with anything listed under the harmonious or discordant side of Pluto.

Spies, secret or foreign agents.

Federal Bureau of Investigation personnel.

Lookouts.

Bootleggers.

Criminals.

Gangsters.

Mobsters.

Gunmen.

Hoodlums.

Crime-busters, cops, police officers.

Fascist, communist.

Terrorist.

Fetishist (also Neptune; Pluto is the obsessed, compulsive and forceful part).

Strikebreaker.

Picketer.

Mediator.

Robber, thief, racketeer.

Pimp, procurer, madam (also Neptune; Pluto is the forceful, co-ercing and illegal part).

Reporters, writers, policemen, detectives or lawyers, or anyone else who does an expose about someone.

One Whose Hobby and/or Work Deals With . . .

Anything listed under the harmonious or discordant side of Pluto.

Collection agencies (threats, harasses and badgering is em-ployed).

Wiretapping, bugging devices.

Pressures, deadlines.

An organized criminal operation systematically exacting tribute from legitimate business (the Mafia).

Extortion of government or any political office (political racketeer).

Extortion of the stock market or financial world (wall street racketeer).

Extortion and shakedown of medicines and drugs by the government (patent medicine rackets).

Underground or undercover work.

Hush-hush work that is illegally performed.

Organized crime (fighting it or on the side of organized crime).

Labor unions.

Socialism, communism.

Organizations.

Companies, corporations.

Branches of a business.

Leagues, bureaus, associations.

Chain store operations.

Fall-out (radio activity in the atmosphere as a result of atomic weapons or devices), nuclear power plants.

Printed in the USA
CPSIA information can be obtained
at www.ICGtesting.com
LVHW041438250124
769628LV00012B/520

9 780866 901369